An Analysis of

Amartya Sen's

Inequality Reexamined

Elise Klein

Published by Macat International Ltd
24:13 Coda Centre, 189 Munster Road, London SW6 6AW.

Distributed exclusively by Routledge
2 Park Square, Milton Park, Abingdon, Oxon OX14 4RN
711 Third Avenue, New York, NY 10017, USA

Routledge is an imprint of the Taylor & Francis Group, an informa business

www.macat.com
info@macat.com

Cataloguing in Publication Data
A catalogue record for this book is available from the British Library.
Library of Congress Cataloguing-in-Publication Data is available upon request.
Cover illustration: Kim Thompson

ISBN 9781912304004 (hardback)
ISBN 9781912284719 (paperback)
ISBN 9781912284856 (e-book)

Notice
The information in this book is designed to orientate readers of the work under analysis,
to elucidate and contextualise its key ideas and themes, and to aid in the development
of critical thinking skills. It is not meant to be used, nor should it be used, as a
substitute for original thinking or in place of original writing or research. References and
notes are provided for informational purposes and their presence does not constitute
endorsement of the information or opinions therein. This book is presented solely for
educational purposes. It is sold on the understanding that the publisher is not engaged
to provide any scholarly advice. The publisher has made every effort to ensure that
this book is accurate and up-to-date, but makes no warranties or representations with
regard to the completeness or reliability of the information it contains. The information
and the opinions provided herein are not guaranteed or warranted to produce particular
results and may not be suitable for students of every ability. The publisher shall not be
liable for any loss, damage or disruption arising from any errors or omissions, or from
the use of this book, including, but not limited to, special, incidental, consequential or
other damages caused, or alleged to have been caused, directly or indirectly, by the
information contained within.

CONTENTS

THE MACAT LIBRARY

The Macat Library is a series of unique academic explorations of seminal works in the humanities and social sciences – books and papers that have had a significant and widely recognised impact on their disciplines. It has been created to serve as much more than just a summary of what lies between the covers of a great book. It illuminates and explores the influences on, ideas of, and impact of that book. Our goal is to offer a learning resource that encourages critical thinking and fosters a better, deeper understanding of important ideas.

Each publication is divided into three Sections: Influences, Ideas, and Impact. Each Section has four Modules. These explore every important facet of the work, and the responses to it.

This Section-Module structure makes a Macat Library book easy to use, but it has another important feature. Because each Macat book is written to the same format, it is possible (and encouraged!) to cross-reference multiple Macat books along the same lines of inquiry or research. This allows the reader to open up interesting interdisciplinary pathways.

To further aid your reading, lists of glossary terms and people mentioned are included at the end of this book (these are indicated by an asterisk [*] throughout) – as well as a list of works cited.

Macat has worked with the University of Cambridge to identify the elements of critical thinking and understand the ways in which six different skills combine to enable effective thinking.
Three allow us to fully understand a problem; three more give us the tools to solve it. Together, these six skills make up the **PACIER** model of critical thinking. They are:

ANALYSIS – understanding how an argument is built
EVALUATION – exploring the strengths and weaknesses of an argument
INTERPRETATION – understanding issues of meaning

CREATIVE THINKING – coming up with new ideas and fresh connections
PROBLEM-SOLVING – producing strong solutions
REASONING – creating strong arguments

To find out more, visit **WWW.MACAT.COM.**

CRITICAL THINKING AND *INEQUALITY REEXAMINED*

Primary critical thinking skill: EVALUATION
Secondary critical thinking skill: REASONING

A key theme in Amartya Sen's *Inequality Reexamined* is the diversity of humanity. Sen argues that humans are all by nature different and so no one measure of any given dimension of (in)equality could ever cover all the things people value or have reason to value. Instead, he proposes the concept of 'capabilities" as a way of understanding inequality.

One of the things that makes *Inequality Reexamined* so powerful is its use of the skill of evaluation as a critical thinking tool. Sen methodically assesses past works that have tried to evaluate inequality. He reviews each of these works, and, while acknowledging their value, also points out their shortcomings within the context of his observation that humans are heterogeneous. Sen then goes on to propose capabilities as an alternative. He does this in well-structured arguments, explaining why his concept is able to deal with this diversity among people. He then applies his concept of capabilities to specific areas such as gender equality, poverty reduction and social welfare to illustrate the applicability of his approach to produce to deliver a well-structured argument that is fit for purpose and without marked weaknesses.

ABOUT THE AUTHOR OF THE ORIGINAL WORK

Amartya Sen was born in 1933 in India. He studied at the Presidency School in Calcutta and University of Cambridge, and has held fellowships at MIT, Harvard University, the London School of Economics and the University of Oxford. He has worked with scholars such as John Rawls, Ronald Dworkin, Anthony Atkinson, Jean Dreze, and Martha Nussbaum. Sen's writings are focused on issues of justice, development, inequality, and poverty reduction. He won won the Nobel Prize for Economics in 1998 for his contribution to welfare economics; the core arguments that won him the prize were developed in *Inequality Reexamined*.

ABOUT THE AUTHOR OF THE ANALYSIS

Dr. Elise Klein holds a PhD from the Department of International Development at the University of Oxford and is a Lecturer of Development Studies at the University of Melbourne. Her research interests include the psy-expertise in development interventions, women's agency, neoliberal subjectivities, economic rights and settler colonialism. Her book, *Developing Minds: Psychology, Neoliberalism and Power*, was recently published by Routledge. She has critically engaged with Sen's capability approach, particularly in regards to agency, Indigenous policy in Australia, and women's empowerment.

ABOUT MACAT

GREAT WORKS FOR CRITICAL THINKING

Macat is focused on making the ideas of the world's great thinkers accessible and comprehensible to everybody, everywhere, in ways that promote the development of enhanced critical thinking skills.

It works with leading academics from the world's top universities to produce new analyses that focus on the ideas and the impact of the most influential works ever written across a wide variety of academic disciplines. Each of the works that sit at the heart of its growing library is an enduring example of great thinking. But by setting them in context – and looking at the influences that shaped their authors, as well as the responses they provoked – Macat encourages readers to look at these classics and game-changers with fresh eyes. Readers learn to think, engage and challenge their ideas, rather than simply accepting them.

'Macat offers an amazing first-of-its-kind tool for interdisciplinary learning and research. Its focus on works that transformed their disciplines and its rigorous approach, drawing on the world's leading experts and educational institutions, opens up a world-class education to anyone.'

Andreas Schleicher
Director for Education and Skills, Organisation for Economic
Co-operation and Development

'Macat is taking on some of the major challenges in university education … They have drawn together a strong team of active academics who are producing teaching materials that are novel in the breadth of their approach.'

Prof Lord Broers,
former Vice-Chancellor of the University of Cambridge

'The Macat vision is exceptionally exciting. It focuses upon new modes of learning which analyse and explain seminal texts which have profoundly influenced world thinking and so social and economic development. It promotes the kind of critical thinking which is essential for any society and economy. This is the learning of the future.'

Rt Hon Charles Clarke, former UK Secretary of State for Education

'The Macat analyses provide immediate access to the critical conversation surrounding the books that have shaped their respective discipline, which will make them an invaluable resource to all of those, students and teachers, working in the field.'

Professor William Tronzo, University of California at San Diego

WAYS IN TO THE TEXT

KEY POINTS

- Amartya Sen is an Indian development philosopher and economist and winner of the 1998 Nobel Prize in Economics.

- *Inequality Reexamined* offers a new way to think about inequality and social arrangements based on Sen's Capability Approach.

- The Capability Approach stands in contrast to other development approaches by including not just economic factors but other aspects of human wellbeing.

Who is Amartya Sen?

Amartya Sen, author of *Inequality Reexamined*, was born in West Bengal, India (now Bangladesh) in 1933. He was born into a family of intellectuals: his maternal grandfather was a prominent Sanskrit* writer and his mother was also a writer; his father was a professor of chemistry. As a young boy, Sen witnessed the suffering of the Bengal famine* in which two to three million people starved to death. The horror of the famine and the obscene loss of life haunted Sen and influenced the direction of his intellectual pursuits and his dedication towards the poor.

Sen has two Bachelor's Degrees in Economics, one from Presidency College in Calcutta, and one from the University of

Cambridge in the United Kingdom. He also received an MA and PhD from Cambridge University.

When he took up his studies for a BA in Economics at Trinity College, Cambridge, Sen found himself surrounded by hotly contested debates between Keynesian economics,* "neo-classical" economics,* and Marxist theory.* It was here that Sen became further interested in working on Social Choice Theory* and Philosophy. It wasn't until some years later when working with the likes of John Rawls,* Ronald Dworkin,* and Anthony Atkinson* in fellowships that would lead him to MIT, Harvard University, the London School of Economics, and the University of Oxford, that his writing became focused on inequality and poverty.

Amartya Sen won the Nobel Prize for Economics in 1998 for his contribution to welfare economics;* the core arguments of this work are set out in *Inequality Reexamined*.

What does *Inequality Reexamined* say?

In his seminal text *Inequality Reexamined*, Amartya Sen asks the question – the *equality of what*? Previous theories of equality had been based on the idea of a specific equality. John Rawls, for example, saw equality as equal liberty and the distribution of such primary goods* as rights, liberty, incomes, wealth, and opportunities. Ronald Dworkin saw equality as the treatment of individuals as equals. This included government that worked to secure a state in which all are equal, with the provision of equal economic resources. Thomas Nagel* also saw equality as economic equality, though with the individual less responsible for their circumstances. Yet, in *Inequality Reexamined*, Sen shows how all of these seminal works focused on equality without addressing the question: the *equality of what*?

There are many different ways in which inequality can be judged and Sen argues that it is important to investigate the specific. According to Sen, "the pervasive diversity of human beings intensifies the need to address the diversity of focus in the assessment of equality."[1] To Sen, the focus on resources can overlook diversity–the heterogeneity* of people–as we are not all born the same. In addition, by focusing only on a particular resource, it isn't clear how someone could transfer such a resource as a personal gain. Because of this diversity between people and the many different possible variables upon which to judge their wellbeing,* Sen argues we then must ask the question: the *equality of what?*

He proposes instead that equality should be assessed as human freedom* and what he calls capabilities.* Sen defines human freedom as not just those things that people have, can be or do (functionings),* but also the ability people have to pursue them in the first place (capabilities).

Sen's case for capabilities as a way to understand equality underpins what is known as the Capability Approach.* This Capability Approach can examine the success of social arrangements not just as economic outputs but in terms of all possible aspects of human flourishing. When capabilities are taken into account, it is possible to measure the achievement and the ability to secure basic needs (resources) as well as life satisfaction, empowerment, and agency.* The multi-dimensional measure of deprivation,* for example, means that countries with high GDPs (Gross Domestic Product)* can be low in other dimensions such as health, education, subjective wellbeing, and gender and sexual equality. For example, Saudi Arabia has a higher GDP than Uganda, yet the mortality rate of women is also higher.[2]

The consideration of capabilities when measuring global inequality has allowed a reconfiguration of deprivation in states across the world. Mahbub ul Haq,* head of the office responsible for writing the "Human Development Report," invited Sen to help develop the very first Human Development Index.* This measure was the first of its kind to measure all nation states on grounds that went beyond income and included life expectancy and education. Later this

11

measure was improved by Sabina Alkire* and James Foster* who created the Multi-Dimensional Poverty Measure* that governments and global institutions can use to measure levels of deprivation other than income such as in education, health and living standards.

Why does *Inequality Reexamined* matter?

Inequality Reexamined challenges orthodox views in economic theory, development, and philosophy that economic growth is the key to human flourishing. Instead, Sen shows through the Capability Approach that people value a much wider range of ways in which their wellbeing can be measured. He includes, for instance, the role of agency and people's ability to choose lives they value or have reason to value, the role of public reasoning and democracy, and the diversity of capabilities people may value.

Many scholars, both within and beyond his field of inequality have praised Amartya Sen's *Inequality Reexamined*. Despite some criticisms, most scholars took the work as a sound basis from which to develop further. The text was viewed largely as an advance in the assessment of social arrangements across the world. Where other academics had tried to define equality from particular philosophical standpoints, Sen's argument called for the need to understand exactly what equality means. This question has broadened the discussion and allowed other factors of human diversity to be included and measured in the conversation about inequality. These include wellbeing, agency, empowerment, subjective wellbeing and a variety of other capabilities and functionings.

Understanding social arrangements as capabilities has had wide implications across the world; specifically in the conceptualization of poverty and deprivation as well as that of development as a whole. Indeed, Sen develops his work on the Capability Approach in *Inequality Reexamined* in his later books, *Development as Freedom* and *The Idea of Justice,* to clarify his positions on capabilities as fundamental to social arrangements.

Scholars and practitioners from many fields have come together under the name of Human Development* in which the Capability Approach is central. The school of human development was born alongside that of the Capability Approach though it does not just focus on the Capability Approach framework. It also includes such theories as basic needs approach, human rights, welfare and development economics,* social psychology, anthropological studies and theories of well-being.

NOTES

1   Amartya Sen, *Inequality Reexamined* (Oxford: Oxford University Press, 1995), 3.

2   Sabina Alkire and Severine Deneulin, *An Introduction to the Human Development and Capability Approach: Freedom and Agency* (London: EarthScan, 2009).

SECTION 1
INFLUENCES

MODULE 1
THE AUTHOR AND THE HISTORICAL CONTEXT

KEY POINTS

- *Inequality Reexamined* is a seminal text in economics, philosophy and development studies.*

- Amartya Sen has held fellowships at the University of Cambridge, MIT, Harvard University, the LSE and the University of Oxford.

- Amartya Sen won the 1998 Nobel Prize in Economics for his work relating to the Capability Approach.

Why Read This Text?

Inequality Reexamined by Amartya Sen is a seminal text on welfare economics and development. The text sets out the ideas fundamental to Amartya Sen's Capability Approach–ideas that have been widely adopted in development economics and the field of human development. Sen argues that development should be examined not only in terms of economic deprivation (not having enough economic resources to fulfill people's basic needs), but also examine development as an expansion of human freedoms. Sen's Capability Approach views human freedoms as not just the achievement of things people value and have reason to value, but also the ability of people to examine such things. This ability or agency is the difference between someone having the freedom to be nourished because they *choose* and *actively pursue* eating particular foods, compared to someone being nourished because they are *forced* to eat particular foods.

Previous intellectuals such as Rawls, Dworkin, and Nagel focused on resources, overlooking the heterogeneity of people and the many

> **❝** Justice cannot be indifferent to the lives that people can actually live. **❞**
>
> Amartya Sen, *The Idea of Justice*

different ways in which equality can be judged. By focusing only on a particular resource of, say, liberty or economic resources, it wasn't clear how a person could transfer such a resource into a gain. Sen concludes: "The heterogeneity of people leads to the divergences in the assessment of quality in terms of different variables. This adds significance to the central question: equality of what?"[1] His argument that inequality was the lack of freedom for people to achieve functionings they valued or had reason to value was widely accepted by the academic community. It was a fascinating perspective for many scholars and policy-makers, moving the debate of inequality away from economics and utility to a broader understanding of human capability, the relevance of which is still central today.

Author's Life

Amartya Sen, the author of *Inequality Reexamined*, was born in 1933 in Bengal, India (now Bangladesh). He is famous for claiming that most of his life has taken place in the grounds of a university. Many of Sen's family were intellectuals, and so it comes as no surprise that he was born in Santiniketan, a small campus just outside of Dhaka.

Sen studied at the Presidency School in Calcutta where he was surrounded by the debates of an intellectual community from Marxist traditions.* His own uncle was a member of the Congress Socialist Party,* who was placed in detention under British rule for six years without trial. Sen went on to Trinity College at the University of Cambridge to study for a BA in Economics. He has subsequently commented on the tolerant nature of Trinity, where economists from extremely different schools of economic thought (neo-classical, Marx, and Keynesian) taught together.

Later, Sen found himself working with the likes of John Rawls, Ronald Dworkin, and Anthony Atkinson, all of whom influenced his thesis in *Inequality Reexamined*. Sen also held fellowships at MIT, Harvard University, the London School of Economics and the University of Oxford. It was in these years that Sen's writings became increasingly focused on measuring inequality and poverty. His work with the philosopher Martha Nussbaum* helped Sen develop his ideas of the Capability Approach.

Author's Background

Diverse social, political, and physical environments influenced the writing of *Inequality Reexamined*. Sen himself has written extensively on the influence of his studies in economics and also social choice theory and philosophy during his time at Trinity College Cambridge, MIT, Harvard University, the London School of Economics and the University of Oxford. In particular, he has commented on how respectful these intellectual environments were of new or competing ideas and how prominent scholars such as Rawls influenced his work. The political theories of Karl Marx and Adam Smith* would also have an effect on his writing.

During his youth, Sen was witness to between two and three million people starving to death in the Bengal famine of 1943. Such personal experiences also contributed to Sen's lifetime's work that would focus on examining and understanding inequality, poverty and development. In his famous essay "Poverty and Famines: An Essay on Entitlement and Deprivation" (1981), he argued that the Bengal famine was not caused by a lack of food. Indeed, at the time, India had enough food. In fact, the famine was caused by a failure in the distribution of resources between different classes. Those that died in the famine were of the landless farming class whose wages could not keep up with the inflation* of food prices.

17

NOTES

1   Amartya Sen, *Inequality Reexamined* (Oxford: Oxford University Press, 1995).

MODULE 2
ACADEMIC CONTEXT

KEY POINTS

- Sen's *Inequality Reexamined* was groundbreaking for academic discussions on inequality.

- *Inequality Reexamined* is an original work emerging from various schools of philosophic inquiry into inequality.

- In *Inequality Reexamined*, Sen draws on scholars from contemporary political philosophy including John Rawls, Ronald Dworkin, and Thomas Nagel.

The Work in its Context

Sen's *Inequality Reexamined* was broke new ground in academic discussions on inequality. The text conceptualized inequality as a lack of capability freedom. It built upon other mainstream analyses at the time of publication, including those that regarded inequality as a lack of resources or utility. *Inequality Reexamined* was written as academic prose, laying out the arguments Sen had already started developing in his seminal work *On Economic Inequality* first published in 1973,[1] and his Tanner "Lectures on Human Values" at Stanford University in 1979, which were later published as the paper "Equality of What?" in 1980.[2]

Sen argues that human diversity is fundamental and no one is born the same. Given this heterogeneity, equality can be judged using many variables. Variables previously used to measure (in)equality, such as resources or utility, are inefficient because they don't account for the ability of people to turn them into gains. For example, if equality was measured by distributing the same amount of food to everyone, it doesn't account for the fact that some people would eat more and

> **66** Equality is confronted by two different types of diversities: 1) the basic heterogeneity (human diversity) of human beings, and 2) the multiplicity of variables in terms of which equality can be judged. **99**
>
> Amartya Sen, *Inequality Reexamined*

others would eat less. This shows why the heterogeneity of people matters when viewing equality and why asking the "equality of what?" is so central.

Overview of the Field

Amartya Sen's *Inequality Reexamined* is an original work emerging from various schools of philosophic inquiry into inequality. Sen particularly acknowledges that his writings are influenced and inspired by the work of several scholars. First, Sen acknowledges John Rawls' *Theory of Justice*. In his early career when Sen was at Harvard University, he taught alongside Rawls. This experience undoubtedly shaped Sen's thinking around inequality. For example, in *Inequality Reexamined*, Sen remarks "While my own approach is deeply influenced by Rawls's analysis, I argue that the particular informational focus on which Rawls himself concentrates neglects some considerations that can be of great importance to the substantive assessment of equality—and also of efficiency."[3]

Sen also draws on Anthony Atkinson, the British economist who focused mainly on welfare economics and issues of inequality. The "Atkinson measure of inequality" has shaped Sen's evaluative arguments as Atkinson, like Sen, challenges assumptions that incomes alone don't determine the level of social welfare experienced by populations.

Karl Marx and his writings on exploitation within capitalism,* were another influence on Sen, who wrote: "The theory of exploitation involved an identification of who is 'producing' what. Exploitation was seen as the enjoyment of one person [the property owner] of the fruits of another's labour."[4] Sen draws on Marx's earlier work on freedom pointing out that Marx saw the need for variation in what defines a person as being free. Specifically Sen writes: "An essential part of Marx's complaint was about the mistake of seeing human beings 'from one definite side only,' in particular seeing people 'only as workers, and nothing more seen in them, everything else being ignored…'" The diversities within the category of the working class made Marx insist on the need to seek other classifications and productivity differences constituted only one of Marx's concerns. He focused attention, too, on the necessity of addressing our many diversities, including differences in needs, and this led him to the well-known slogan "from each according to his ability to each according to his needs."[5] Sen has contributed in debates regarding market* and non-market forces, and between private and public action, though he has been critiqued for not taking a direct position on capitalism in his work.[6]

Sen also acknowledges the influence of Adam Smith* and his work in *An Inquiry into the Nature and Causes of the Wealth of Nations (1776)*. Adam Smith's earlier philosophical writings in these two texts establish the importance of markets* (institutions that facilitate trade and exchange between peoples) to operate freely in order to create wealth. Although referred to fleetingly in *Inequality Reexamined,* Smith's writings have influenced Sen's arguments especially in regards to Smith's understanding of the inherent variation of an individual's capabilities.

Academic Influences

In *Inequality Reexamined*, Sen draws on scholars from contemporary political philosophy including John Rawls, Ronald Dworkin, and Thomas Nagel. At the time of writing *Inequality Reexamined*, these scholars were prominent thinkers in debates on (in)equality. John Rawls is an American political and moral philosopher most famous for his life's work expounded in the book *Theory of Justice*. This book became central to legal theories and analyses of inequality. Rawls views equality/inequality as liberty in the distribution of primary goods (such as incomes, wealth and opportunities). Ronald Dworkin is an American philosopher of constitutional law, justice, and equality. Dworkin viewed equality as the treatment of all individuals as equals and equality of resources. Thomas Nagel completed his PhD at Harvard University under the supervision of John Rawls is a political liberal philosopher. He saw equality as economic equality.

The works by Rawls, Dworkin and Nagel gave Sen the departure point for his writings on inequality. he reviewed carefully the arguments put forward by each of these scholars, concluding that they each defined equality by something – resource (such as money), utility (such as happiness), liberty (such as freedom). Sen found this insufficient because people are not all the same and have diverse needs – hence his proposal that we must raise the question, the *equality of what?*

NOTES

1   Amartya Sen, *On Economic Inequality* (Oxford: Oxford University Press, 1973).

2   Amartya Sen, "*Equality of What? Tanner Lecture on Human Values,*" Stanford University.

3   Amartya Sen, *Inequality Reexamined* (Oxford: Oxford University Press), 8.

4   Sen, *Inequality Reexamined*, 118-119.

5   Sen, *Inequality Reexamined*, 120.

6   Andrew Sayer, "Capabilities, contributive injustice and unequal divisions of labour." *Journal of Human Development and Capabilities* 13, no. 4 (2012), 580-596.

MODULE 3
THE PROBLEM

KEY POINTS

- Sen shows how seminal works at the time of *Inequality Reexamined* focused on equality without asking: the equality of what?

- Sen argues that human diversity is fundamental to understanding (in)equality.

- Sen moves existing debates on inequality away from viewing it as just a problem of the distribution of utility, resource or liberty.

Core Question

Sen shows how seminal works at the time of writing *Inequality Reexamined* focused on the question of equality without asking the question, the *equality of what*?

His emphasis is on the importance of human diversity. Given this heterogeneity, he believes equality should be judged using a diverse array of variables. When Sen was writing his book, however, the variables used to measure (in)equality were limited to resources, liberty or utility. According to Sen, these were not enough because they didn't account for the ability of people to turn them into achievements. So, even if people received them, they may not value them or choose to use them.

Sen illustrates his point with the example of two people. The firs person has an income level lower than second, but the second person has a kidney problem and needs to use a dialysis machine that costs a lot of money and leads him to live an impoverished life. Sen's question is:

> 66 The pervasive diversity of human beings intensifies the need to address the diversity of focus in the assessment of equality. 99
>
> Amartya Sen, *Inequality Reexamined*

who then is most poor? Is it the first person because he has less money or the second because he has less capability and lives a restricted life? The difficulty in answering such a question is the reason Sen argues that to measure inequality simply in terms of resources is inefficient.

Measures of utility present a similar problem. Utility as a mental metric of happiness, pleasure or desire is a very narrow understanding of individual wellbeing. To illustrate its limitations, Sen uses the example of someone in a state of chronic grieving. Instead of pining for the impossible all the time (bringing the beloved back to life), it is better to try to enjoy small breaks. Such a person, argues Sen "even though thoroughly deprived and confined to a very reduced life, may not appear to be quite so badly off in terms of the mental metric of desire and its fulfillment … The extent of a person's deprivation may be substantially muffled in the utility metric, despite the fact that he or she may lack the opportunity even to be adequately nourished, decently clothed, minimally educated or properly sheltered."[1]

These problems provoke Sen to ask, *the equality of what*?

The Participants

Amartya Sen's main aims in *Inequality Reexamined* were to move the then existing debates on inequality away from viewing it as a problem merely of distribution of utility, resource or liberty. He builds his argument from an examination of John Rawls's work who saw equality as equal liberty (freedom) and equality in the distribution of primary goods. Ronald Dworkin, on the other hand, viewed equality as the treatment of individuals as equals and equality of resources while Thomas Nagel described it in terms of economic equality. Sen respectfully acknowledges the important contributions of these scholars and their theses but builds on their work so that equality can include the diverse preferences, aspirations, and realities around the world. He thus propounds a more complete definition.

In *Inequality Reexamined*, Sen proposes that equality should be understood as human capabilities that are diverse and heterogeneous and depend on social and cultural contexts as well as individual differences. Indeed, to Sen human freedom is understood as capabilities–as not just the *achievement* of things people value or have reason to value, but also the *ability* of people to examine them in the first place.

The Contemporary Debate

In *Inequality Reexamined*, Sen carefully walks the reader through the failures of previous theories of inequality. He explains that these previous theories fall short because they don't identify the variables that account for human diversity when analyzing inequality.

Sen proceeds to illustrate for the reader the need to understand the distinction between achievement of specific variables (or what he calls functionings), and the freedom choose them in the first place. This distinction between ability and achievement, he says, should lie at the very heart of all assessments of inequality: while many look at what has been achieved (freedoms people may or may not have), few look at the process by which these freedoms came about.

This is where Sen's capability approach thesis enters. Sen proposes a view of inequality based on people's capability or "ability" to achieve being or doing something one values or has reason to value. In doing so, he moves the debate away from discussions just of economic inequality to other aspects important for human flourishing. For example, inequality in happiness, freedom of movement, and inequality in gender relations.

Sen then shows how his capability approach can be used in various distinct areas of study such as poverty and social welfare analysis where deprivation can be understood in terms of people's ability or inability to live lives they value or have reason to value.

NOTES

1   Sen, *Inequality Reexamined*, 7.

MODULE 4
THE AUTHOR'S CONTRIBUTION

KEY POINTS

- Amartya Sen advances the thinking on inequality by introducing the idea of human freedom into the debate.

- Sen aims to reconcile and extend contemporary understandings of human freedom to include capabilities.

- *Inequality Reexamined* is the seminal distillation of decades of Sen's work.

Author's Aims

By asking the question, the "equality of what?" Amartya Sen aims to reconcile the limitations of previous approaches that specified specific variables in the measurement of equality and to include capabilities in the contemporary understanding of human freedom. In moving the debate away from these specific variables, Sen brings in the diversity and plurality of the human condition.

Sen understands human freedom as not just the achievement of things people can be or do (functionings), but the freedom or ability to pursue them in the first place (capabilities). Capabilities are diverse and can capture many aspects of human life: the ability to be happy to to have basic needs met, the ability to move freely, to love whom you wish, and to have spiritual expression.

There are two new approaches in *Inequality Reexamined*. Firstly, a framework on equality should allow for the diversity in all the things people may value or have reason to value. Secondly, the role of human agency and choice is central to compiling context specific lists of capabilities. Sen proposes the importance of public debate and

> ❝ A person's position in a social arrangement can be judged in two different perspectives 1) the actual achievement, and 2) the freedom to achieve. Achievement is concerned with what we manage to accomplish, and freedom with the real opportunity that we have to accomplish what we value. The two need to be congruent. ❞
>
> Amartya Sen, *Inequality Reexamined*

democracy: each group can, through reasoning and deliberation, come up with its own list of valued capabilities to define equality.

Approach

Sen's central thesis is that equality should be assessed as human freedoms where these are not just the *achievement* of functionings people value or have reason to value but also the *ability* that people have to examine them in the first place. Sen arrives at his core argument through a review of earlier writings on moral and political philosophy of inequality, specifically those of Ronald Dworkin and John Rawls, Thomas Nagel and Tomas Scanlon.*

Sen defines a gap in the thinking of earlier approaches to inequality. He convincingly outlines how they have overlooked two very important aspects of assessing inequality. The first concerns human diversity: it is inegalitarian to expect all people to be treated as equals because we are not. The second considers the resulting multiplicity of variables that we can use to assess inequality.

Sen moves the intellectual framework of the time forward by introducing an idea of human freedom that addresses the shortfalls of the old view of inequality. To Sen, freedom is understood as not just the achievement of things that a person values or has reason to value, but also the ability to achieve these things (capability).

Contribution in Context

In *Inequality Reexamined* Sen proposes the original idea that past assessments of inequality are inefficient. He has continued to use the insights in *Inequality Reexamined* and develop them further throughout his career. He draws on many schools of thought to illustrate this point, that issoundly and firmly rooted in the work of Marx, Rawls, Smith, and Atkinson.

Sen's writings complement other human development and people-centered approaches such as the Basic Needs Approach.* The Basic Needs Approach focuses on the need for the minimum quantities of food, shelter, water and sanitation necessary to prevent ill health or undernourishment. However, unlike capabilities, basic needs rely both on the ability of individuals to transform these items into personal gain, and the environment they live in. For example, the basic commodities required for someone to be in good health and not undernourished is not just about how much food is available. Factors such as climate and physiological characteristics are also relevant. As Sen points out, basic needs do not give sufficient attention to agency and freedoms.

In 1990, Sen wrote a controversial article in *The New York Review of Books* called "More Than 100 Million Women Are Missing."This essay argued that because of the inequality of women in India, their mortality rate was unacceptably higher than that of men. Sen estimated that, because women lacked the capability to access such necessities as food, health care and education, they died early and this amounted to 100 Million women missing in the Indian population.

SECTION 2
IDEAS

MODULE 5
MAIN IDEAS

KEY POINTS

- *Inequality Reexamined* is based on the themes of human diversity and inequality, human freedom, capabilities and functionings, and human agency.

- Amartya Sen's notion of freedom has two elements; the opportunity that a person has, and the process that achieves freedom.

- The Capability Approach has been widely applauded, though its inner theoretical workings can be misunderstood.

Key Themes

Inequality Reexamined by Amartya Sen can be understood through four themes: human diversity; freedom; capabilities and functionings; and human agency.

Sen addresses human diversity in his argument that, in previous theories of equality, the heterogeneity of people didn't feature. Given we are not all born the same, Sen says, there are many different ways in which equality can be judged. Sen's contribution to this debate is the introduction of capabilities as the key aspect of evaluating equality.

Sen's definition of human freedom underpins his contribution to the Capability Approach. The Capability Approach assesses human freedom not just by the *achievement* of certain functionings (what people can do, be, have), but also the *ability* they have to pursue these functionings (capabilities).

Ability refers here to the agency people have to act and choose those capabilities they value. This agency component is a fundamental

> 66 A person's capability to achieve functionings that he or she has reason to value provides a general approach to the evaluation of social arrangements, and this yields a particular way of viewing the assessment of equality and inequality. 99
>
> Amartya Sen, *Inequality Reexamined*

addition to the understanding of inequality. Sen also uses the concept of agency as a way to compile context specific lists of valued capabilities and these capabilities should, he says, be discussed, debated and reasoned by people across a society.

Sen provides an extensive and exhaustive analysis of functionings, capabilities and agency in *Inequality Reexamined*. He goes on to apply this approach to inequality to substantive social challenges. Specifically, Sen discusses the Capability Approach regarding issues of justice, poverty and affluence, welfare economics and class and gender.

Exploring the Ideas

Sen's idea of freedom is fundamental to improving the assessment of inequality. In *Inequality Reexamined* Sen says, that freedom has two elements. Opportunity freedom is the availability of functionings that the individual values or has reason to value. Process freedoms* are the means whereby people achieve these functionings or capability.

We can understand functionings in terms of what people can be or do: being nourished, educated, healthy or riding a bike. The capability is the *ability* to achieve these functionings (the ability to be nourished, the ability to be educated, the ability to be healthy). Functionings may come as a group of capabilities. For example, the ability to go to school may include the functionings of having transport, having finances to pay for school fees, books and uniform as well as having access to a school.

The difference between capabilities and functionings also relates to the process or agency, whereby someone achieves a state or thing. So undernourishment could be the result of an extreme diet aimed at losing weight or because of a famine in the village. This example shows that the process of becoming undernourished can involve both agency and choice and this is fundamental in assessing someone's freedom and wellbeing.

Sen's Capability Approach is underpinned by the concept of agency. To Sen, agency is the ability to act on whatever a person values. Agency is not the same as wellbeing even though wellbeing may be the focus and aim of most individual agency. This is not, though, always the case. Some people may jeopardize wellbeing, Sen says, to achieve "other regarding goals" or goals that aren't about maximizing personal wellbeing. For example, a man may risk his life to save the life of someone who has just fallen overboard from a ship. This is a rejection of any rational theory notion that humans act only for maximizing personal wellbeing.

Nonetheless, Sen maintains that there should be some evaluation of society's view of agency. Clearly, people cannot just pursue whatever actions they like – such as maiming other people. This is why public reasoning or discussion on the subject should be included in any given social context.

There is a difference between the way Sen uses the concepts of ability and achievement that can take some time to grasp. According to Sen, wellbeing achievement is the actualization of goals specific to one's own personal wellbeing. Agency achievement, however, is the realization of goals that may or may not be in line with one's personal wellbeing goals but in line with their agency goals – such as saving someone falling overboard from a ship. Wellbeing freedom is the ability to pursue goals for personal wellbeing. Agency freedom is the ability to pursue goals in a fuller sense, not necessarily for one's own wellbeing. An extreme version of this agency freedom is the ability to end one's own life.

In *Inequality Reexamined*, Sen focuses on the virtues of both the individual and of democratic society (process freedoms at both individual and collective levels). This is central to compiling evaluative lists of capabilities and Sen's discussion about public reasoning and democracy.

Language and Expression

Sen seamlessly raises his ideas and themes, allowing them to emerge organically through a well thought-out text. He walks the reader through the themes central to his argument in a logical pattern, first by presenting the current theoretical landscape of inequality as problems, then by discussing at length his amendments and solutions. Finally, Sen applies his Capability Approach to various social issues to cement their relevance in debates on equality. Understanding social arrangements as capabilities has had wide implications across the world, specifically in the conceptualization of poverty and deprivation as well as in development.

The Capability Approach has been widely acclaimed. Its inner theoretical workings, however, can be misunderstood, particularly in terms of the language Sen uses in the Capability Approach. Terms such as capabilities, human freedoms, process freedoms, opportunity freedoms, agency and functionings can sometimes be tricky to appreciate and decipher as it is specific jargon. As a result, most people outside the scholarly debates, policy and research find *Inequality Reexamined* confusing and difficult to fully understand despite it being relevant to social arrangements around the world. Nonetheless, *Inequality Reexamined* is written clearly, Sen being praised as a thorough, wonderful and engaging writer.

MODULE 6
SECONDARY IDEAS

KEY POINTS

- Amartya Sen shows that, when equality is understood as capabilities, equality and liberty are not in opposition with each other.

- Democracy and collective process freedoms are also important to Sen.

- Sen applies the capability framework to distinct areas of inquiry such as class analysis, gender analysis, poverty and social welfare.

Other Ideas

There are several important secondary ideas in *Inequality Reexamined*.

One of these is that equality and liberty are not in opposition to each other, when equality is understood through capabilities. This is an important contribution to the academic literature on this subject that had previously viewed equality and liberty as being in competition. This earlier argument regards equality as one specific variable (such as income or utility), leaving the individual without the freedom to choose his or her own idea of what is valuable. Moreover, the freedom of an individual to pursue a specific end may come at a cost of someone else's equality. For example, one person might pursue the mass acquisition of land in the name of liberty, leaving someone else without access to land.

Sen's understanding of democracy and collective process freedoms is also important. It is vital, he says, that when any society attempts to come up with a list of capabilities, public reasoning and deliberation on the matter should be central. Sen places a high value on democracy in the Capability Approach.

> ❝ Even the freedom-based perspective must pay particular attention to the nature and value of the actual achievements, and inequalities in achievement can throw light on inequalities in the respective freedoms enjoyed. ❞
>
> Amartya Sen, *Inequality Reexamined*

Exploring the Ideas

Sen begins with the idea that equality and liberty are not opposites. They can, in fact, coexist when they are based on an assessment of capabilities. In classical political theory texts, equality and liberty are presented as concepts in competition with each other. The argument is that when equality is viewed as specific variables (such as income or utility), it can impinge on someone's freedom to choose what variable really is important. Furthermore, where one individual pursues a specific variable in the name of liberty, it may conflict with equality of others (the accumulation of capital in the name of freedom comes at the expense of the equality of others). However, this is no longer the case when freedom is viewed as capabilities, as both freedom and equality are based on capabilities that people value or have reason to value. Sen states, "Liberty is among the possible fields of application of equality, and equality is among the possible patterns of distribution of liberty."[1] Thus within the full Capability Approach, including public deliberation, both are possible.

Sen's interpretation of democracy and collective process freedoms are also important to his thesis. Capabilities are central to his work, and so too are the roles of agency and democratic freedoms in the process of developing and compiling any list of capabilities. Sen maintains that for any such list to be developed, it must be context specific and involve public deliberation about what capabilities should be valued and included.

Overlooked

Although Sen's *Inequality Reexamined* has provided a useful tool for the evaluation of inequality, Sen seldom makes any explicit comments regarding structural oppression or the role of capitalism in creating inequality. This has led to an ambiguity about Sen's own views on Marx's critique of capitalism.

Sen does draw on Marx to discuss class and he specifies the importance of class analysis in examining inequality. His argument is that class analysis is important because it "indicate[s] why it is the case the equality in the space of say, libertarian rights does not yield anything like equality of well-being or equality of the overall freedoms to lead the lives that people may respectively value. They also draw attention to the importance of inequalities in wealth and income in generating unequal well-beings and living conditions, even when there is equality in formal procedures an in the allocation of some specific facilities."[2]

Nonetheless, Sen argues that class should never be the only focus of inequality. He draws from Marx himself to show that "An essential part of Marx's complaint was about the mistake of seeing human beings from one definite side only, in particular seeing people only as workers, and nothing more seen in them, everything else being ignored."[3]

NOTES

1   Amartya, Sen, *Inequality Reexamined* (Oxford, Oxford University Press, 1995), 22-23.

2   Sen, *Inequality Reexamined*, 118.

3   Sen, *Inequality Reexamined*, 120.

MODULE 7
ACHIEVEMENT

KEY POINTS

- Amartya Sen, through *Inequality Reexamined*, has been successful in reframing debates about inequality and development more broadly.

- The *United Nations Development Program** and the *World Bank** are two institutions that use the language of capabilities regularly in their policies and evaluations.

- A challenge for the Capability Approach is how to compile context specific lists that are reasoned publically.

Assessing the Argument

Sen's arguments in *Inequality Reexamined*, have been successful in reframing debates about inequality and development more broadly.

Sen examines the widespread tool used to measure inequality – the poverty line. To Sen, the use of this line and particularly the cut off can be problematic. Not only does the poverty line take account only of economic deprivation, it also fails to include other forms of deprivation. Furthermore, the poverty line fails to account for the poorer of the poor, that is the difference in deprivation between people who are just below the poverty line compared to those well below it.

By taking capabilities into account, one can measure the achievement and the ability to secure basic needs as well as life satisfaction, empowerment, and agency.

Sen's capabilities have been applied across different contexts in many parts of the world. The Capability Approach as an evaluative mechanism has revealed deprivation in rich countries as well as poor ones. This is a distinguishing feature of the Capability Approach.

> **❝** If poverty is seen as the deprivation of some minimum fulfillment of elementary capabilities, it becomes easier to understand why it has both an absolute and relative aspect. These considerations are important in dealing with poverty in any country (rich and poor), but are particularly relevant in understand in the nature of poverty in richer countries. **❞**
>
> Amartya Sen, *Inequality Reexamined*

Other measures of inequality, such as those based on resources, divide rich and poor nation states but don't provide enough information about other forms of deprivation that rich nation states may be experiencing.

Evaluation has also gone beyond the political boundaries of nation states to look at regional populations, for instance looking at deprivation levels across different regions of India.

Achievement in Context

The consideration of capabilities when measuring global inequality has meant that economic measures such as GDP are not the only ones considered when assessing levels of deprivation in states across the world. This has made it possible not only to conceptualize a fuller notion of inequality but also to measure it.

The *United Nations Development Program* and the *World Bank* are two institutions that use the language of capabilities regularly in their policies and evaluation. Specifically, Mahbub-ul-Haq* head of the office responsible for writing the *Human Development Report*,* invited Sen to help develop the very first Human Development Index (HDI).* This was the first of its kind to measure all nation states on grounds that went beyond income and included changing levels of human deprivation across the domains of living standards, education and life expectancy. The HDI was a huge improvement to those measures based more restrictively on income.

Later the HDI measure was improved by Sabina Alkire* and James Forster* who created the *Multi Dimensional Poverty Measure*. States and global institutions can use this instead of income measures to show levels of deprivation in domains other than income, such as education, living standards, and health. The MPI has the capacity to include other domains for measurement such as safety and empowerment (something that the HDI does not do).

Limitations

A challenge to the Capability Approach is how collective public reasoning can be used in compiling context specific and relevant lists. Specifically, capabilities should be discussed, debated and reasoned by people across a society to achieve a set of virtues and values acceptable to them. The process and practicality of compiling such lists is complex and true democracy needs to be in place if all voices are to be heard and acknowledged.

Sen's definition of democracy goes beyond that of political theorist Robert Dahl,* who narrowly defines it as access to information and ballot boxes. Instead, Sen sees democracy in much broader terms that include people's ability to access public debate, have similar levels of education so they can understand and engage in the topics being deliberated, and have access to a free and effective media to aid communication.

While this view of democracy is admirable, in reality it is seldom found, and all societies have some groups of people more privileged than others. In both rich and poor countries, it is difficult for such public reasoning to occur and oppressive structures create power struggles and marginalized peoples across the world. The limitation of the Capability Approach is that, until a true form of democracy is

MODULE 8
PLACE IN THE AUTHOR'S WORK

KEY POINTS

- *Inequality Reexamined* is a text that has served as an important foundation for further debate.

- Amartya Sen has further developed his arguments on the Capability Approach in *Development as Freedom* (1999) and *the Idea of Justice* (2009).

- Sen's ideas on inequality, development and justice have proved very useful across many academic disciplines.

Positioning

Amartya Sen won the Nobel Prize for Economics in 1998 for his contribution to welfare economics. The core arguments of this work are made in *Inequality Reexamined*.

Many of Sen's writings before and after *Inequality Reexamined* show the application of his approach to a variety of social, welfare and developmental issues such as poverty reduction, development of countries, gender discrimination and measurement. While a seminal text in itself, *Inequality Reexamined* was expanded upon in some of Sen's later that clarify his Capability Approach. Writings that came after *Inequality Reexamined* include *Development and Freedom* and *The Idea of Justice*, both clarifying and expanding on points he set out in *Inequality Reexamined*. Sen's main argument has not changed and the clarifications and extensions he has subsequently made have further strengthened his arguments and the impact of the Capability Approach. The corpus of Sen's work has thus been highly influential and remains so to this day.

> **"** Human beings are not merely means of production,
> but also the end of the exercise. **"**
>
> Amartya Sen, *Development as Freedom*

Sen with Martha Nussbaum and others founded the *Human Development and Capabilities Association** which acts as a forum for critiques and improvements to current debates regarding the Capability Approach. The association focuses on work in the field of human development to which the Capability Approach is central. The association includes scholars from many different fields of enquiry including academics and policy-makers.

Integration

Sen has continued developing and rearticulating his arguments made in *Inequality Reexamined* in various books and journal articles. The corpus of Sen's work is published in diverse disciplinary outlets but retains a clarity and coherence. The key arguments made in *Inequality Reexamined* continue through Sen's later work.

Soon after *Inequality Reexamined* was published Sen began working on *Development as Freedom (1999).* This later book seeks to redefine our understanding of development beyond mere economic development. Instead, Sen uses arguments around capabilities developed in *Inequality Reexamined* to define development as capabilities and the ability of people to live lives they value or have reason to value. *Development as Freedom* is a seminal text in development studies. In its explanation of development as a multidimensional process rather than a simple economic one, it has left a lasting impact on both scholars and practitioners.

Sen continued his work on capabilities in *The Idea of Justice* (2009). Here, he further developed his ideas about the role of democracy and public reasoning and how capabilities relate to philosophies of rights and the law. Sen sees a human rights based approach and the capability approach as mutually reinforcing. While there are indeed many human rights* that may be essential to achieving particular capabilities (such as political and economic rights), human rights alone do not necessarily guarantee process freedoms (some rights can be forced on people). Consequently, Sen suggests that the capabilities framework is complementary to the human rights one because it specifically focuses on processes, freedoms and agency.

Sen's work is vast both in terms of volume and disciplinary application. However, it is worth students continuing to read him beyond *Inequality Reexamined* because he engages with critiques of his work and has gained clarity in his arguments and reasoning. By seeing how Sen applies his Capability Approach to a broad array of situations and his engagement in diverse disciplinary debates, one gains not only a greater appreciation of the skill and care of his writing, but the importance of the Capability Approach to scholarship.

Significance

Sen's ideas on inequality, development and justice have proved very useful across many disciplines. The Capability Approach relates to a wide variety of functionings and capabilities central to human flourishing and wellbeing–not just resources and utility. This approach has been game changing in the academic analysis of inequality, development and human agency and has fuelled wider debates about the purpose of development. The practical applications of the Capability Approach have also been revolutionary in the field of those practitioners 'doing' development.

Inequality Reexamined was the beginning of Sen's rise to fame and he developed many of his ideas further in subsequent works. Not long after the publication of *Inequality Reexamined*, Sen won the Nobel Prize for the contribution the Capability Approach made to welfare economics.

There has been critical engagement with the Capability Approach, but its central premise is widely acknowledged as fundamental within the social sciences. Sen himself has constructively engaged in criticism – using it as a forum of public reasoning. Each new development in his work continues to clarify, evolve and expand his original ideas through the substantive issues of our time.

The Capability Approach is important in its contribution towards realizing a possible world beyond the current paradigm where societies are evaluated on resources and capital. This entails moving towards a deeper consideration of human freedoms and the ability of people to realize lives they value.

SECTION 3
IMPACT

MODULE 9
THE FIRST RESPONSES

KEY POINTS

- Context specific lists need to be complied through public reasoning to enable an assessment of capabilities. This can be difficult.

- Martha Nussbaum, to help with the difficulty in compiling lists, has proposed 10 universal capabilities.

- Amartya Sen continues to dispute the idea of compiling any universal list of capabilities.

Criticism

With such groundbreaking ideas and claims, it was inevitable that Amartya Sen's *Inequality Reexamined* drew a lot of critical attention. This was mainly focused on three areas.

The first critique of *Inequality Reexamined* argued that it showed a lack of practicality in its Capability Approach. This criticism questioned whether context specific lists of capabilities could ever be compiled in real life situations given the difficulty in getting the information needed to measure such capabilities and that of compiling relevant sets of capabilities in the first place. Fellow academic Martha Nussbaum argued that "Sen needs to be more radical than he has been so far ... by introducing an objective normative account of human functioning and by describing a procedure of objective evaluation by which functionings can be assessed for their contribution to the good human life."[1] Nussbaum, in her book *Women and Human Development,* went on to compile a list of *10 Universal Human Capabilities* and suggested they could be used as a pragmatic solution to this criticism. These capabilities are as follows:

❝ The problem is not with listing important capabilities, but with insisting on one pre-determined list of capabilities, chosen by theorists without any general or public reasoning. To have such a fixed list, emanating entirely from pure theory, is to deny the possibility of fruitful public participation on what should be included and why. ❞

Amartya Sen, *Human Rights and Capabilities*

1. Life: being able to live to the end of a human life of normal length; not dying prematurely or a life so reduced as to be not worth living.
2. Bodily health: being able to have good health, including reproductive health; to be adequately nourished; to have adequate shelter.
3. Bodily integrity: being able to move freely from place to place; to be secure against violent assault, including sexual assault and domestic violence; having opportunities for sexual satisfaction and for choice in matters of reproduction.
4. Senses, imagination, and thought: being able to use the senses, to imagine, think, and reason—and to do these things in a truly human way, a way informed and cultivated by an adequate education.
5. Emotions: being able to have attachments to things and people outside ourselves; to love those who love and care for us, to grieve at their absence; in general, to love, to grieve, to experience longing, gratitude, and justified anger.
6. Practical reason: being able to form a concept of good and to engage in critical reflection about the planning of one's life.

7. Affiliation:
   a. being able to live with others, and
   b. having the social bases of self-respect and non-humiliation.
8. Other species: being able to live with concern for and in relation to animals, plants, and the world of nature.
9. Play: being able to laugh, to play, to enjoy recreational activities.
10. Control over one's political and material environment.[2]

One critique that Sen makes himself points to the incompleteness of the Capability Approach. He argues that for an assessment of capabilities, context specific lists need to be complied through public reasoning. Yet for this to take place, the apparatus of true democracy needs to be in place where all people, if they desire, can engage in the process. For Sen, democracy includes the ability to engage in public reasoning, which can rely on a free and effective media.

The unit of analysis in Sen's work is the individual and the last major criticism by Francis Stewart* and Séverine Deneulin* is that his focus is too individualistic and should account more for collective capabilities and collective agency. Sen does include the importance of collective processes such as democracy and public reasoning in his work. Solava Ibrahim* has written on the concept of collective capabilities in the Capability Approach.

The work of Ingrid Robeyns,* one of Sen's student's reveals some of the common misunderstandings of the Capability Approach. Robyens demonstrates the difference between evaluative individualism, ontological* individualism and explanatory individualism. According to ontological individualism, human society is explained as the sum of all individuals and their properties (society is nothing but individuals). Explanatory individualism sees all social phenomena in terms of individuals and their properties (all things happen because of human action). Evaluative individualism focuses solely on the individual so there is some form in which to describe and analyze. Sen's Capability

Approach uses evaluative individualism as an analytical mechanism, but goes beyond it with the understanding that the individual is not the only phenomenon in society.

Responses

Sen has responded extensively to critiques of *Inequality Reexamined* and related works. Soon after *Inequality Reexamined* was published he set to work on *Development as Freedom*. This text aimed to develop his ideas about the role of democracy and public reasoning, the pursuit of human freedom and the realization of the Capability Approach. Sen built on this discussion in *The Idea of Justice,* with substantive arguments that showed the wide applicability of his conception of freedom. He continues to develop these ideas to this day.

Sen acknowledges the incompleteness of the Capability Approach given that some people are more privileged than others and so more able to engage in democratic processes. However, he argues that the presence of power imbalances caused by race, class or gender is not reason enough to abandon his ideas–we cannot wait until perfect institutions are established to solve such imbalances. Instead, Sen says that the "success of democracy is not merely a matter of having the most perfect institutional structure that we can think of. It depends inescapably on our actual behaviour patterns and the working of political and social interactions. There is no chance of resting the matter in the 'safe' hands of purely institutional virtuosity. The working of democratic institutions, like that of all other institutions, depends on the activities of human agents in utilising opportunities for reasonable realisation."[3]

Conflict and Consensus

The initial critiques that followed the publication of *Inequality Reexamined* continue to challenge the Capability Approach today. Specifically, there is the ongoing perceived difficulty of the practicality of getting sufficient information to measure specific capabilities and also the difficulty in compiling relevant sets of capabilities in the first place (how to democratically compile context specific lists of capabilities). Sen in his continuing writing has tried to address these various critiques—and this is a challenge that other scholars have picked up through the Human Development and Capability Association.

Sen to this day disputes the idea of compiling any universal list of capabilities and argues they should always be created in context specific situations where options are democratically reasoned, debated and discussed in and with the people. Debate also continues between the Sen camp and the Nussbaum camp as to the pros and cons of the universal list of capabilities. Some pragmatic thinkers feel that Nussbaum's list of capabilities is better than having nothing at all. They worry that without endorsing the Nussbaum list, policy makers may dismiss the Capability Approach altogether because it is not easy to implement. Others, though, have worked with policy makers including Sen himself to help develop context specific lists of capabilities.

NOTES

1   Martha Nussbaum, "Nature, Function, and Capability: Aristotle on Political Distribution," in *Oxford Studies in Ancient Philosophy: Supplementary Volume* (Oxford: Oxford University Press, 1988), 145-184.

2   Martha Nussbaum, *Women and Human Development: The Capabilities Approach* (Cambridge, UK: Cambridge University Press, 2000).

3   Amartya Sen. *The Idea of Justice* (London: Allen Lane, 2009), 354.

MODULE 10
THE EVOLVING DEBATE

KEY POINTS

- Amartya Sen's core thesis of capabilities has contributed to the founding of the Human Development school of thought.

- The Capability Approach has contributed to various academic theories and disciplines.

- Scholars currently contributing to the Capability Approach include Anthony Atkinson, Tomas Pogge,* Frances Stewart and James Foster.

Uses and Problems

Since writing *Inequality Reexamined*, Sen's focus has increasingly been on promoting human wellbeing and reducing human deprivation. Specifically, he has written extensively on issues of human development, democracy and justice on a global level as well as in specific contexts such as his country of birth, India.

Sen's core thesis of capabilities has contributed to the founding of the Human Development school of thought—for which the Capability Approach underpins most scholarly enquiry. Human development has been taken up by other development scholars throughout institutions such as the UNDP* and their annual Human Development reports dating back to 1990. Human development can be typified by two attributes. Firstly, it puts humans in the centre of all development processes (unlike the growth paradigm which has capital at its centre). Secondly, it is multi-dimensional and includes the many capabilities needed for human development.

> ❝ The relative advantages and disadvantages that people have, compared with each other, can be seen in many different perspectives, involving different concentrations, e.g. liberties, rights, incomes, wealths, resources, primary goods, utilities, capabilities, and so on, and the question of inequality assessment turns on the selection of the space in which equality is to be assessed. ❞
>
> Amartya Sen, *Inequality Reexamined*

Sen's writings on democracy, especially those on the importance of public reasoning as well as creating lists of capabilities, have been also important. With Jean Drèze,* Sen has applied his approach to India, discussing issues such as child malnutrition, women's high mortality rates when compared to those of men, human rights and unemployment.

Schools of Thought

The Capability Approach has contributed to various academic theories and disciplines including social choice theory, welfare economics, economic measurement, development economics, philosophy, development studies, social policy, human development, political theory, legal theory, and sociology. Scholars critically engaging with the Capability Approach have done so not to undermine it but in the spirit of enhancing and developing it for wider applicability. Indeed, Sen's writings have been important for many of the social sciences.

Sen's work has also been taken up by policy makers and practitioners. Scholars forming the *Human Development and Capability Association* have worked hard to build bridges to ensure that mainstream policy and practitioners do not overlook his approach. Specifically, the *United Nations Development Program* and the *World*

Bank have picked up on applications of the Capability Approach through their policies and measures of social and economic progress. Many governments around the world have also tried to integrate measures of multi-dimensional development rather than just economic measures. The *Human Development Index, Multi Dimensional Poverty Measure* and many empirical and theoretical studies by scholars have helped in this.

All of these initiatives are particularly important in keeping Sen's main arguments in *Inequality Reexamined* on the table. These are ideas that are central to human functioning and flourishing, but they can be deemed too difficult to put into action, or are not given priority by neo-liberal governments that focus on economic growth rather than human development.

In Current Scholarship

Scholars from a wide range of disciplines across the social sciences working on issues of development, justice and political economy are familiar with the Capability Approach. They include Anthony Atkinson, Tomas Pogge, Frances Stewart, James Foster, Sabina Alkire, Peter Singer*, Martha Nussbaum and Ingrid Robeyns.

These scholars use Sen's work in significantly different ways. Most have commented on the applicability of the central thesis to their fields of study. For example, Thomas Pogge has shown how the Capability Approach is helpful in the field of global health while Peter Singer has drawn on capabilities in the field of ethics and development. Others have critically examined the work its contribution to wider philosophical arguments. These include Anthony Atkinson on inequality measurement, Frances Stewart on horizontal inequalities (inequalities across groups) and Martha Nussbaum on gender and operationalizing the capability approach.

Sen is active in many debates on the Capability Approach and regularly engages with authors across the social science disciplines. As a scholar of economics as well as philosophy and political theory, he has been able to engage constructively with the writings of other scholars. This dialogue has enabled the Capability Approach to mature and innovate through empirical and theoretical dialogue.

MODULE 11
IMPACT AND INFLUENCE TODAY

KEY POINTS

- The theory and application of the Capability Approach are still very relevant today.
- The Capability Approach stands in contrast to other development approaches that see human beings as merely the means to economic growth.
- Some scholars have suggested that caution must be applied in the application of collective process freedoms such as deliberation and democracy.

Position

Amartya Sen's arguments in *Inequality Reexamined* remain relevant today. Critical debates about his work have clarified the Capability Approach and become more robust. These discussions and related empirical research have also allowed the approach to be applied to many social problems. Sen himself continues to engage in debates about his work and clarifies points in his later writings such as *Development as Freedom* and *The Idea of Justice*. In addition, there are many scholars such as Sabina Alkire and James Foster working on issues Sen has raised in *Inequality Reexamined*. These works by scholars other than Sen add to the empirical and theoretical debates.

Other writers also focus not just on the ability of governments and other institutions to compile lists of capabilities, but also the ability to collect the data needed to measure capabilities. The work of Sabina Alkire and James Foster has been extremely useful in this pursuit, allowing for easier implementation of the Capability Approach by providing a tool with the capacity to measure capability deprivation at

> ❝ A space in which evaluation is to take place, rather than proposing one particular formula for evaluation. ❞
>
> Amartya Sen, *The Concept of Development*

a global level. Even so, it is still difficult to collect actual household level data on certain capabilities because not all countries have the resources to be able to collect such internationally comparable information.

Interaction

According to the Capability Approach, economic advancement is only pursued as a means. The ends are human wellbeing. This approach is in stark contrast to other normative development approaches that see human beings as means to economic growth. Capabilities are the freedoms people have to undertake doings and beings (functionings) they value and have reason to value. Consequently, economic and social policy should exist only as a way to expand the actual freedoms people have, not to decide which freedoms people experience.

Some governments and policy-makers can reduce humans to mere labor and key aspects of "the economy." However, according to the Capability Approach, capabilities should not be restricted to what is necessary for economic growth. Instead, the capabilities that people value are the very things that are most vital to human flourishing and these may or may have a capitalist or economic function.

The capability approach was not, though, created as a theory to explain social phenomena. Rather, it was purposefully designed to evaluate and conceptualize social phenomena, complementing other disciplinary perspectives. As a result, the capability approach itself has no specific theory of political economy and so it can be misused to support the neoliberal tendency to acknowledge social structures and power in the shaping of people's lived reality.

The Continuing Debate

Sen has an implicit concern with power relations and unjust social structures. He does not, however, make an explicit analysis of capitalism and how it relates to inequality. Caution must, therefore, be applied when considering collective process freedoms such as deliberation and democracy—because some people are more privileged than others. The racialized, gendered and economic constitution of society tends to structure the options that individuals have and can exclude some groups or give them more rights or entitlements than others even within democratic processes. While some people have immense privilege, others are oppressed due to their class, race or gender. Moreover, these unjust relations of power and social structures can be reproduced through collective process freedoms, where the very act of engaging in deliberation or democratic processes can oppress people further. At a protest, for example, liberal feminists may talk over women of color, or within collective action, men may exclude women, or rich owners of media outlets may distort the news in favour of their interests.

Critical social theories could remedy such a dilemma and complement the capability approach given their specific focus on power relations and the structural conditions of individual and collective agency. However, leaving scholars and policy makers to decide whether or not to engage in critical social theories to complement the capability approach, "creates scope for more casual and indeed opportunistic appropriations and interpretations"[1].

NOTES

1   Andrew Sayer, "Capabilities, contributive injustice and unequal divisions of labour," *Journal of Human Development and Capabilities* 13, no. 4 (2012): 582.

MODULE 12
WHERE NEXT?

KEY POINTS

- Amartya Sen's arguments are central to fundamental issues concerning the flourishing of humanity and society.
- Many contemporary scholars continue to build on his work.
- *Inequality Reexamined* lays out the fundamental ideas to Sen's work on the Capability Approach.

Potential

It is highly likely that in the future the arguments raised by Amartya Sen in *Inequality Reexamined* will remain relevant in many areas of social change and progress. Sen's arguments are, in fact, central to fundamental issues concerning the flourishing of humanity and society. For example, the Capability Approach is currently used to examine issues such as gender equality, environmental degradation, poverty, democracy, justice, economic systems, human rights and economic development.

The Capability Approach isn't new to development policy, but with the increased focus on the importance of human agency and inequality, these two fundamental concepts are likely to gain more prominence in mainstream development policy and practice. This would contribute to a shift away from social arrangements based on profit and accumulation to ones that place greater value on human flourishing and equality. It would also encourage policy makers to make people central to decisions where agency is central to freedom and equality.

Continuing theoretical and empirical research is needed to work through challenges to the Capability Approach and help its theoretical and practical application. This is especially important for the practical

> **❝** Social arrangements should be primarily evaluated according to the extent of freedom people have to promote or achieve functionings they value. Put simply, progress, or development, or poverty reduction, occurs when people have greater freedoms. **❞**
>
> Sabina Alkire, *Using the Capability Approach: Prospective and Evaluative Analyses*

integration of capabilities into mainstream policy and also in addressing issues of existing power imbalances that keep public debate limited and somewhat overlooked.

Future Directions

Amartya Sen has many followers who use his writings and arguments in *Inequality Reexamined* and elsewhere in their own scholarly research. Such scholars include Solava Ibrahim, Séverine Deneulin, and Frances Stewart, James Foster, Sabina Alkire and Ingrid Robeyns. These writers are all working on the ideas of Amartya Sen but come from a wide range in disciplines and interests.

Development studies scholar, Solava Ibrahim, has developed ideas on collective capabilities, arguing that groups, as well as individuals, have capabilities. Francis Stewart has developed the concept of horizontal inequalities,* which looks at inequalities such as ethnicities across groups. Political philosopher, Séverine Deneulin, works on the ethics of the Capability Approach, specifically examining possible issues of paternalism arising in its application. Economist Sabina Alkire has been instrumental in helping policy makers and academics make more practical use of the Capability Approach. Specifically, she has worked with James Foster in creating the Multi Dimensional Poverty measure, which expands on the existing Human Development Index to provide internationally comparable measures of human capabilities. The work of Ingrid Robeyns has also been important in outlining a procedure for selecting capabilities to help with the practical application of the Capability Approach. The work of all of these scholars and others has greatly enhanced our knowledge of inequality.

Summary

Amartya Sen's *Inequality Reexamined* is a seminal text in welfare economics and international development literature and puts forward the fundamental ideas of Amartya Sen's Capability Approach. These have been celebrated in development economics and the field of human development. Sen's aim is to show that poverty is not only about economic deprivation and that development should be an expansion of human freedoms not income or utility.

The contribution of Sen in his writings of *Inequality Reexamined* is twofold. He begins with the question—the *equality of what?* Until Sen's writings, all theories of inequality of social arrangements were based on a specific variable, usually a utility or resource. In *Inequality Reexamined*, Sen shows how such past seminal works focused on the equality of *something* without asking the question of equality of *what?*

Secondly, because a particular variable was previously used to measure inequality, it overlooked the heterogeneity of people and the many different ways in which equality can be evaluated. To reconcile these issues, Sen proposed the Capability Approach. Equality should be assessed, he said, as human freedom where that is understood not just as *achievement* of functionings that people value or have reason to value, but also the *ability* to pursue them in the first place (capabilities).

The Capability Approach is important and will continue to be fundamental in the contribution towards realizing a world where a society's value is based not on resources and capital, but on human freedoms and the ability of individuals to lives where they can flourish.

GLOSSARY

GLOSSARY OF TERMS

Agency: human action, the ability to act and/or choose.

Basic Needs Approach: the need to attain some minimum specified quantities of food, shelter, water and sanitation necessary to prevent ill health or undernourishment and support life.

Bengal famine: the famine in Bengal, India, in which two to three million people starved to death in 1943.

Capability: the ability to achieve things people value or have reason to value (the ability to be nourished, the ability to be educated, the ability to be healthy and so on).

Capitalism: an economic system in which transactions are carried out through markets, facilitated by the investment of capital by private individuals. Within capitalism, there is a division between who owns the means of production/wealth creation and the workers.

Congress Socialist Party: a socialist caucus of the Indian National Congress founded in 1934.

Deprivation: living without specific basic needs, functionings or capabilities.

Development economics: a sub-discipline of economics focusing on issues of development, traditionally in the Global South.

Development Studies: an interdisciplinary field of scholarship examining issues of development and economic and social change.

Explanatory individualism: a theory that all social phenomena can be understood in terms of individuals and their properties (all things happen because of human action).

Evaluative individualism: a theory that focuses on the individual only as a unit of analysis to describe and analyse social phenomena.

Functionings: actual beings and doings (being nourished, riding a bike, being educated or healthy).

Freedom: the ability to live a life you value or have reason to value.

Gross Domestic Product: the measure of economic development of a specific country based on the total value of goods and services produced.

Heterogeneity: the word Sen uses to describe human diversity and the inherent differences among human beings.

Horizontal inequalities: the study of inequalities across groups.

Human Development: a field that was born alongside the Capability Approach. Human development does not just focus on the Capability Approach framework, it integrates other theories such as basic needs approach, human rights, welfare and development economics, social psychology, anthropological studies and theories of well-being to name just a few.

Human Development and Capabilities Association (HDCA): a forum for critiques and improvements to current debates regarding the Capability Approach.

Human Development Index: a multidimensional measure of development including life expectancy, education, and living standards.

Human Development Report: an annual publication of the United Nations Development Programme that measures various aspects of human development, including income, environmental sustainability, gender equality, and education.

Human rights: a set of moral principles describing standards of human behavior that are protected by international law.

Inflation: an economic term referring to the increase in prices and fall of purchasing value of money.

Keynesian economics: theories of economic governance associated with the British economist John Maynard Keynes. Keynesians traditionally believe that the government can help to mitigate the relationship between labour and capital. They also believe they can stabilize an economy in the event of financial crises by supplementing private spending with public spending.

Markets: the institutions that organize economic behavior between willing sellers of goods and willing buyers. An alternative economic system would be to allow governments to set prices.

Marxist theory: a collection of ideas and theories relating to the work of Karl Marx including the labor theory of value, dialectical materialism, the class struggle and the practice of socialism.

Multi Dimensional Poverty Measure: a formula for measurement that states and global institutions can use instead of income measures to show levels of deprivation.

Neoclassical economics: an approach to economics, often contrasted with Keynesian economics, that seeks to understand economic behavior through an analysis of market institutions and the establishment of prices.

Neoliberalism: a term often used negatively to describe a perspective on economic development that emphasizes the liberalization of markets and sosical structures that benefits capital and oppresses labor.

Ontological individualism: a theory that explains human society only as the sum of all individuals and their properties (society is nothing but individuals).

Opportunity Freedoms: the first aspect of Sen's notion of freedom that includes the real opportunities and achievements people have.

Primary goods: goods useful and desirable for all human beings set out by John Rawls in his *A Theory of Justice* (1971). Primary goods are in two categories; natural primary goods such as intelligence, imagination, and health; and social primary goods including rights (civil rights and political rights), incomes, wealth, and opportunities.

Process Freedoms: the second aspect of Sen's notion of freedom that includes the way in which outcomes are achieved. Process freedoms include agency and democratic processes such as public deliberation.

Sanskrit: an ancient language of India, in which classical Indian poems are written and from which the Hindu language has evolved.

Social Choice Theory: a subfield of economics concerned with understanding how preference aggregation rules, such as voting, can translate individual beliefs into rational group action. Kenneth Arrow's impossibility theorem is a key result.

The Capability Approach: a way of assessing social arrangements not just by the *achievement* of certain functionings (what people can do, be, have), but also the *ability* by which they can purse these functionings.

The World Bank: an international organization founded in 1944. The World Bank has controversially played a central role in implementing economic reforms in developing countries since its creation.

United Nations Development Program: an agency of the United Nations mandated to focus on issues of development.

Utility: a word defined by Sen to refer to an individual and general mental characteristic, such as pleasure, happiness or desire.

Welfare economics: a subfield of economics concerned with how economic well-being is created and distributed throughout society.

Wellbeing: the status of human flourishing.

PEOPLE MENTIONED IN THE TEXT

Sabina Alkire is the director of the Oxford Human Development Initiative at the Department of International Development at the University of Oxford. She was a founding member of the Human Development and Capabilities Association and has published widely on the measurement of capabilities.

Anthony Atkinson (b. 1944) is a British economist focusing mainly on welfare economics and issues of inequality. Atkinson is a Fellow at the University of Oxford and a Professor at the London School of Economics.

Robert Dahl (1915-2014) was an American political scientist and Professor Emeritus of political science at Yale University. Dahl has written several seminal works on democracy and political pluralism including *Who Governs? Democracy and Power in an American City* (1961).

Séverine Deneulin (b. 1974) is a lecturer in human development and ethics at the University of Bath, and a fellow of the Human Development as Capability Association.

Jean Drèze (b. 1959) is a Belgian-born economist who has written extensively on human development issues with Amartya Sen. He is currently an Honorary Professor at the Delhi school of Economics.

Ronald Dworkin (1931–2013) was an American philosopher of constitutional law, justice and equality who viewed equality as the treatment of individuals as equals and with equality of resources. He studied at the University of Oxford as a Rhodes Scholar and became Professor of Law and Philosophy at New York University and Emeritus Professor at University College London.

James Foster (b. 1955) is a Professor of Economics and International Affairs at the Elliott School of International Affairs at the George Washington University. His current work focuses on using such economic tools as the Multi Dimensional Poverty Measure to evaluate people's wellbeing.

Solava Ibrahim is an affiliated lecturer at the Centre of Development Studies at University of Cambridge. Her work examines collective capabilities using the capability approach.

John Maynard Keynes (1883–1946) was a British economist who had a major influence on academic economics and policy. He is perhaps best known for describing how governmental interventions in the economy during times of crisis may reduce the magnitude of the crisis.

Karl Marx (1818–1883) was a political economist and philosopher born into a wealthy family in Prussian Germany. Marx studied at the Universities of Bonn and Berlin and lived in Paris and London. His influential writings included an unsurpassed critique of capitalism still proving relevant today.

Thomas Nagel (b. 1937) is currently University Professor of Philosophy and Law Emeritus at New York University. He completed his PhD under the supervision of John Rawls and has written extensively against Neo-Darwinist movements, rejecting the idea of natural selection, arguing that humans have consciousness.

Martha Nussbaum (b. 1947) is a philosopher and the Ernst Freund Distinguished Service Professor of Law and Ethics at the University of Chicago. She writes extensively on the capability approach in which she has worked closely with Amartya Sen and also Roman philosophy, feminism and animal rights.

Tomas Pogge (b. 1953) is a German philosopher who is currently Leitner Professor of Philosophy and International Affairs at Yale University. He completed his PhD at Harvard University under John Rawls.

John Rawls (1921–2002) was a famous political and moral philosopher most famous for his life's work bound into the book "Theory of Justice." This book became central to legal theories and analysis of inequality. Rawls studied at the University of Oxford and was a professor at Harvard University.

Thomas Scanlon (b. 1940) was the Alford Professor of Natural Religion, Moral Philosophy, and Civil Polity at Harvard University. His writings deal with moral philosophy, especially issues of justice and equality.

Peter Singer (b. 1946) is a moral philosopher and activist. He is Ira W. DeCamp Professor of Bioethics at Princeton University and a Laureate Professor at the Centre for Applied Philosophy and Public Ethics at the University of Melbourne.

Adam Smith (1723–1790) is considered to be the founding father of Enlightenment political economy. His magnum opus is *An Inquiry into the Nature and Causes of the Wealth of Nations* (1776).

Frances Stewart (b. 1940) is an Emeritus Professor at the Department of International Development and Director of the Centre for Research on Inequality, Human Security and Ethnicity (CRISE) at the University of Oxford. His publications include *Horizontal Inequalities and Conflict: Understanding Group Conflict in Multiethnic Societies* (2008) and *War and Underdevelopment* (2001)

Mahbub ul Haq (1934–98) was a Pakistani economist who assisted with the creation of the human development theory and the Human Development Index.

WORKS CITED

WORKS CITED

Alkire, Sabina. *Valuing Freedoms: Sen's Capability Approach and Poverty Reduction*. Oxford: Oxford University Press, 2002.

— "Using the Capability Approach: Prospective and Evaluative Analyses." *The Capability Approach: Concepts, Measures and Applications*, edited by Flavio Comim and Mozaffar Qizilbash. Cambridge: Cambridge University Press, 2008: 26-50.

Alkire, Sabina, and Severine Deneulin. *An Introduction to the Human Development and Capability Approach: Freedom and Agency*. London: EarthScan, 2009.

Alkire, Sabina, and James Foster. "Understandings and Misunderstandings of Multidimensional Poverty Measurement." *Journal of Economic Inequality,* 9 (2011): 289-314.

Atkinson, Anthony. "On the Measurement of Inequality." *Journal of Economic Theory,* 2 (1970): 244-263.

Dahl, Robert. *Democracy and its Critics*. New Haven, CT: Yale University, 1989.

Dworkin, Ronald. *Taking Rights Seriously*, 2nd edn. London, Duckworth: 1978.

— "'What is Equality? Part 1: Equality of Welfare', and 'What is Equality? Part 2: Equality of Resources'." *Philosophy and Public Affairs,* 10, no 4 (1981): 283-345.

Marx, Karl. *The Economic and Philosophic Manuscript of 1844*. English trans. London, Lawrence and Wishart: 1844.

Nagel, Thomas. *Mortal Questions*. Cambridge, Cambridge University Press: 1979.

— *The View from Nowhere*. New York, Oxford University Press, 1986.

Nussbaum, Martha. "Nature, Function, and Capability: Aristotle on Political Distribution" *Oxford Studies in Ancient Philosophy* (1988): 145-184.

— *Women and Human Development: The Capabilities Approach*. Cambridge, UK: Cambridge University Press, 2000.

— "Nature, Function, and Capability: Aristotle on Political Distribution." *Oxford Studies in Ancient Philosophy: Supplementary Volume*. Oxford: Oxford University Press, 1988: 145-184.

Rawls, John. *A Theory of Justice*. Cambridge, USA: Harvard University Press, 1971.

— "Priority of Right and Ideas of the Good." *Philosophy and Public Affairs,* 17, no. 4 (1988): 251-276.

Robyens, Ingrid. "Sen's Capability Approach and Gender Inequality: selecting relevant capabilities." *Feminist Economics,* 9, no. 2 (2003): 61-92.

— "The Capability Approach: a Theoretical Survey." *Journal of Human Development,* 6, no. 1 (2005): 93-117.

Sayer, Andrew. "Capabilities, contributive injustice and unequal divisions of labour." *Journal of Human Development and Capabilities* 13, no. 4 (2012): 580-596.

Scanlon, Tomas. *Notes on Equality.* Cambridge, USA: Harvard University, 1988.

Sen, Amartya. *On Economic Inequality.* Oxford, Oxford University Press, 1973.

— *Equality of What? Tanner Lecture on Human Values.* Stanford University, 1979.

— *Poverty and Famines: An Essay on Entitlement and Deprivation.* Oxford: Oxford University Press, 1981.

— "The Concept of Development." *Handbook of Development Economics,* edited by Hollis Burnley-Chenery and T.N. Srinivasan. Oxford: Elsevier, 1988.

— *Inequality Reexamined.* Oxford, Oxford University Press, 1995.

— *Development as Freedom.* Oxford: Oxford University Press, 1999.

— "Human Rights and Capabilities." *Journal of Human Development* 6, no. 2 (2005): 151-166.

— *The Idea of Justice,* London: Allen Lane, 2009.

Smith, Adam. *An Inquiry into the Nature and Causes of the Wealth of Nations.* London: Home University, 1910 [1776].

The Theory of Moral Sentiments. Oxford: Clarendon Press, 1975 [1790].

THE MACAT LIBRARY
BY DISCIPLINE

AFRICANA STUDIES

Chinua Achebe's *An Image of Africa: Racism in Conrad's Heart of Darkness*
W. E. B. Du Bois's *The Souls of Black Folk*
Zora Neale Huston's *Characteristics of Negro Expression*
Martin Luther King Jr's *Why We Can't Wait*
Toni Morrison's *Playing in the Dark: Whiteness in the American Literary Imagination*

ANTHROPOLOGY

Arjun Appadurai's *Modernity at Large: Cultural Dimensions of Globalisation*
Philippe Ariès's *Centuries of Childhood*
Franz Boas's *Race, Language and Culture*
Kim Chan & Renée Mauborgne's *Blue Ocean Strategy*
Jared Diamond's *Guns, Germs & Steel: the Fate of Human Societies*
Jared Diamond's *Collapse: How Societies Choose to Fail or Survive*
E. E. Evans-Pritchard's *Witchcraft, Oracles and Magic Among the Azande*
James Ferguson's *The Anti-Politics Machine*
Clifford Geertz's *The Interpretation of Cultures*
David Graeber's *Debt: the First 5000 Years*
Karen Ho's *Liquidated: An Ethnography of Wall Street*
Geert Hofstede's *Culture's Consequences: Comparing Values, Behaviors, Institutes and Organizations across Nations*
Claude Lévi-Strauss's *Structural Anthropology*
Jay Macleod's *Ain't No Makin' It: Aspirations and Attainment in a Low-Income Neighborhood*
Saba Mahmood's *The Politics of Piety: The Islamic Revival and the Feminist Subject*
Marcel Mauss's *The Gift*

BUSINESS

Jean Lave & Etienne Wenger's *Situated Learning*
Theodore Levitt's *Marketing Myopia*
Burton G. Malkiel's *A Random Walk Down Wall Street*
Douglas McGregor's *The Human Side of Enterprise*
Michael Porter's *Competitive Strategy: Creating and Sustaining Superior Performance*
John Kotter's *Leading Change*
C. K. Prahalad & Gary Hamel's *The Core Competence of the Corporation*

CRIMINOLOGY

Michelle Alexander's *The New Jim Crow: Mass Incarceration in the Age of Colorblindness*
Michael R. Gottfredson & Travis Hirschi's *A General Theory of Crime*
Richard Herrnstein & Charles A. Murray's *The Bell Curve: Intelligence and Class Structure in American Life*
Elizabeth Loftus's *Eyewitness Testimony*
Jay Macleod's *Ain't No Makin' It: Aspirations and Attainment in a Low-Income Neighborhood*
Philip Zimbardo's *The Lucifer Effect*

ECONOMICS

Janet Abu-Lughod's *Before European Hegemony*
Ha-Joon Chang's *Kicking Away the Ladder*
David Brion Davis's *The Problem of Slavery in the Age of Revolution*
Milton Friedman's *The Role of Monetary Policy*
Milton Friedman's *Capitalism and Freedom*
David Graeber's *Debt: the First 5000 Years*
Friedrich Hayek's *The Road to Serfdom*
Karen Ho's *Liquidated: An Ethnography of Wall Street*

John Maynard Keynes's *The General Theory of Employment, Interest and Money*
Charles P. Kindleberger's *Manias, Panics and Crashes*
Robert Lucas's *Why Doesn't Capital Flow from Rich to Poor Countries?*
Burton G. Malkiel's *A Random Walk Down Wall Street*
Thomas Robert Malthus's *An Essay on the Principle of Population*
Karl Marx's *Capital*
Thomas Piketty's *Capital in the Twenty-First Century*
Amartya Sen's *Development as Freedom*
Adam Smith's *The Wealth of Nations*
Nassim Nicholas Taleb's *The Black Swan: The Impact of the Highly Improbable*
Amos Tversky's & Daniel Kahneman's *Judgment under Uncertainty: Heuristics and Biases*
Mahbub Ul Haq's *Reflections on Human Development*
Max Weber's *The Protestant Ethic and the Spirit of Capitalism*

FEMINISM AND GENDER STUDIES

Judith Butler's *Gender Trouble*
Simone De Beauvoir's *The Second Sex*
Michel Foucault's *History of Sexuality*
Betty Friedan's *The Feminine Mystique*
Saba Mahmood's *The Politics of Piety: The Islamic Revival and the Feminist Subject*
Joan Wallach Scott's *Gender and the Politics of History*
Mary Wollstonecraft's *A Vindication of the Rights of Women*
Virginia Woolf's *A Room of One's Own*

GEOGRAPHY

The Brundtland Report's *Our Common Future*
Rachel Carson's *Silent Spring*
Charles Darwin's *On the Origin of Species*
James Ferguson's *The Anti-Politics Machine*
Jane Jacobs's *The Death and Life of Great American Cities*
James Lovelock's *Gaia: A New Look at Life on Earth*
Amartya Sen's *Development as Freedom*
Mathis Wackernagel & William Rees's *Our Ecological Footprint*

HISTORY

Janet Abu-Lughod's *Before European Hegemony*
Benedict Anderson's *Imagined Communities*
Bernard Bailyn's *The Ideological Origins of the American Revolution*
Hanna Batatu's *The Old Social Classes And The Revolutionary Movements Of Iraq*
Christopher Browning's *Ordinary Men: Reserve Police Batallion 101 and the Final Solution in Poland*
Edmund Burke's *Reflections on the Revolution in France*
William Cronon's *Nature's Metropolis: Chicago And The Great West*
Alfred W. Crosby's *The Columbian Exchange*
Hamid Dabashi's *Iran: A People Interrupted*
David Brion Davis's *The Problem of Slavery in the Age of Revolution*
Nathalie Zemon Davis's *The Return of Martin Guerre*
Jared Diamond's *Guns, Germs & Steel: the Fate of Human Societies*
Frank Dikotter's *Mao's Great Famine*
John W Dower's *War Without Mercy: Race And Power In The Pacific War*
W. E. B. Du Bois's *The Souls of Black Folk*
Richard J. Evans's *In Defence of History*
Lucien Febvre's *The Problem of Unbelief in the 16th Century*
Sheila Fitzpatrick's *Everyday Stalinism*

Eric Foner's *Reconstruction: America's Unfinished Revolution, 1863-1877*
Michel Foucault's *Discipline and Punish*
Michel Foucault's *History of Sexuality*
Francis Fukuyama's *The End of History and the Last Man*
John Lewis Gaddis's *We Now Know: Rethinking Cold War History*
Ernest Gellner's *Nations and Nationalism*
Eugene Genovese's *Roll, Jordan, Roll: The World the Slaves Made*
Carlo Ginzburg's *The Night Battles*
Daniel Goldhagen's *Hitler's Willing Executioners*
Jack Goldstone's *Revolution and Rebellion in the Early Modern World*
Antonio Gramsci's *The Prison Notebooks*
Alexander Hamilton, John Jay & James Madison's *The Federalist Papers*
Christopher Hill's *The World Turned Upside Down*
Carole Hillenbrand's *The Crusades: Islamic Perspectives*
Thomas Hobbes's *Leviathan*
Eric Hobsbawm's *The Age Of Revolution*
John A. Hobson's *Imperialism: A Study*
Albert Hourani's *History of the Arab Peoples*
Samuel P. Huntington's *The Clash of Civilizations and the Remaking of World Order*
C. L. R. James's *The Black Jacobins*
Tony Judt's *Postwar: A History of Europe Since 1945*
Ernst Kantorowicz's *The King's Two Bodies: A Study in Medieval Political Theology*
Paul Kennedy's *The Rise and Fall of the Great Powers*
Ian Kershaw's *The "Hitler Myth": Image and Reality in the Third Reich*
John Maynard Keynes's *The General Theory of Employment, Interest and Money*
Charles P. Kindleberger's *Manias, Panics and Crashes*
Martin Luther King Jr's *Why We Can't Wait*
Henry Kissinger's *World Order: Reflections on the Character of Nations and the Course of History*
Thomas Kuhn's *The Structure of Scientific Revolutions*
Georges Lefebvre's *The Coming of the French Revolution*
John Locke's *Two Treatises of Government*
Niccolò Machiavelli's *The Prince*
Thomas Robert Malthus's *An Essay on the Principle of Population*
Mahmood Mamdani's *Citizen and Subject: Contemporary Africa And The Legacy Of Late Colonialism*
Karl Marx's *Capital*
Stanley Milgram's *Obedience to Authority*
John Stuart Mill's *On Liberty*
Thomas Paine's *Common Sense*
Thomas Paine's *Rights of Man*
Geoffrey Parker's *Global Crisis: War, Climate Change and Catastrophe in the Seventeenth Century*
Jonathan Riley-Smith's *The First Crusade and the Idea of Crusading*
Jean-Jacques Rousseau's *The Social Contract*
Joan Wallach Scott's *Gender and the Politics of History*
Theda Skocpol's *States and Social Revolutions*
Adam Smith's *The Wealth of Nations*
Timothy Snyder's *Bloodlands: Europe Between Hitler and Stalin*
Sun Tzu's *The Art of War*
Keith Thomas's *Religion and the Decline of Magic*
Thucydides's *The History of the Peloponnesian War*
Frederick Jackson Turner's *The Significance of the Frontier in American History*
Odd Arne Westad's *The Global Cold War: Third World Interventions And The Making Of Our Times*

LITERATURE

Chinua Achebe's *An Image of Africa: Racism in Conrad's Heart of Darkness*
Roland Barthes's *Mythologies*
Homi K. Bhabha's *The Location of Culture*
Judith Butler's *Gender Trouble*
Simone De Beauvoir's *The Second Sex*
Ferdinand De Saussure's *Course in General Linguistics*
T. S. Eliot's *The Sacred Wood: Essays on Poetry and Criticism*
Zora Neale Huston's *Characteristics of Negro Expression*
Toni Morrison's *Playing in the Dark: Whiteness in the American Literary Imagination*
Edward Said's *Orientalism*
Gayatri Chakravorty Spivak's *Can the Subaltern Speak?*
Mary Wollstonecraft's *A Vindication of the Rights of Women*
Virginia Woolf's *A Room of One's Own*

PHILOSOPHY

Elizabeth Anscombe's *Modern Moral Philosophy*
Hannah Arendt's *The Human Condition*
Aristotle's *Metaphysics*
Aristotle's *Nicomachean Ethics*
Edmund Gettier's *Is Justified True Belief Knowledge?*
Georg Wilhelm Friedrich Hegel's *Phenomenology of Spirit*
David Hume's *Dialogues Concerning Natural Religion*
David Hume's *The Enquiry for Human Understanding*
Immanuel Kant's *Religion within the Boundaries of Mere Reason*
Immanuel Kant's *Critique of Pure Reason*
Søren Kierkegaard's *The Sickness Unto Death*
Søren Kierkegaard's *Fear and Trembling*
C. S. Lewis's *The Abolition of Man*
Alasdair MacIntyre's *After Virtue*
Marcus Aurelius's *Meditations*
Friedrich Nietzsche's *On the Genealogy of Morality*
Friedrich Nietzsche's *Beyond Good and Evil*
Plato's *Republic*
Plato's *Symposium*
Jean-Jacques Rousseau's *The Social Contract*
Gilbert Ryle's *The Concept of Mind*
Baruch Spinoza's *Ethics*
Sun Tzu's *The Art of War*
Ludwig Wittgenstein's *Philosophical Investigations*

POLITICS

Benedict Anderson's *Imagined Communities*
Aristotle's *Politics*
Bernard Bailyn's *The Ideological Origins of the American Revolution*
Edmund Burke's *Reflections on the Revolution in France*
John C. Calhoun's *A Disquisition on Government*
Ha-Joon Chang's *Kicking Away the Ladder*
Hamid Dabashi's *Iran: A People Interrupted*
Hamid Dabashi's *Theology of Discontent: The Ideological Foundation of the Islamic Revolution in Iran*
Robert Dahl's *Democracy and its Critics*
Robert Dahl's *Who Governs?*
David Brion Davis's *The Problem of Slavery in the Age of Revolution*

Alexis De Tocqueville's *Democracy in America*
James Ferguson's *The Anti-Politics Machine*
Frank Dikotter's *Mao's Great Famine*
Sheila Fitzpatrick's *Everyday Stalinism*
Eric Foner's *Reconstruction: America's Unfinished Revolution, 1863-1877*
Milton Friedman's *Capitalism and Freedom*
Francis Fukuyama's *The End of History and the Last Man*
John Lewis Gaddis's *We Now Know: Rethinking Cold War History*
Ernest Gellner's *Nations and Nationalism*
David Graeber's *Debt: the First 5000 Years*
Antonio Gramsci's *The Prison Notebooks*
Alexander Hamilton, John Jay & James Madison's *The Federalist Papers*
Friedrich Hayek's *The Road to Serfdom*
Christopher Hill's *The World Turned Upside Down*
Thomas Hobbes's *Leviathan*
John A. Hobson's *Imperialism: A Study*
Samuel P. Huntington's *The Clash of Civilizations and the Remaking of World Order*
Tony Judt's *Postwar: A History of Europe Since 1945*
David C. Kang's *China Rising: Peace, Power and Order in East Asia*
Paul Kennedy's *The Rise and Fall of Great Powers*
Robert Keohane's *After Hegemony*
Martin Luther King Jr.'s *Why We Can't Wait*
Henry Kissinger's *World Order: Reflections on the Character of Nations and the Course of History*
John Locke's *Two Treatises of Government*
Niccolò Machiavelli's *The Prince*
Thomas Robert Malthus's *An Essay on the Principle of Population*
Mahmood Mamdani's *Citizen and Subject: Contemporary Africa And The Legacy Of Late Colonialism*
Karl Marx's *Capital*
John Stuart Mill's *On Liberty*
John Stuart Mill's *Utilitarianism*
Hans Morgenthau's *Politics Among Nations*
Thomas Paine's *Common Sense*
Thomas Paine's *Rights of Man*
Thomas Piketty's *Capital in the Twenty-First Century*
Robert D. Putman's *Bowling Alone*
John Rawls's *Theory of Justice*
Jean-Jacques Rousseau's *The Social Contract*
Theda Skocpol's *States and Social Revolutions*
Adam Smith's *The Wealth of Nations*
Sun Tzu's *The Art of War*
Henry David Thoreau's *Civil Disobedience*
Thucydides's *The History of the Peloponnesian War*
Kenneth Waltz's *Theory of International Politics*
Max Weber's *Politics as a Vocation*
Odd Arne Westad's *The Global Cold War: Third World Interventions And The Making Of Our Times*

POSTCOLONIAL STUDIES

Roland Barthes's *Mythologies*
Frantz Fanon's *Black Skin, White Masks*
Homi K. Bhabha's *The Location of Culture*
Gustavo Gutiérrez's *A Theology of Liberation*
Edward Said's *Orientalism*
Gayatri Chakravorty Spivak's *Can the Subaltern Speak?*

PSYCHOLOGY

Gordon Allport's *The Nature of Prejudice*
Alan Baddeley & Graham Hitch's *Aggression: A Social Learning Analysis*
Albert Bandura's *Aggression: A Social Learning Analysis*
Leon Festinger's *A Theory of Cognitive Dissonance*
Sigmund Freud's *The Interpretation of Dreams*
Betty Friedan's *The Feminine Mystique*
Michael R. Gottfredson & Travis Hirschi's *A General Theory of Crime*
Eric Hoffer's *The True Believer: Thoughts on the Nature of Mass Movements*
William James's *Principles of Psychology*
Elizabeth Loftus's *Eyewitness Testimony*
A. H. Maslow's *A Theory of Human Motivation*
Stanley Milgram's *Obedience to Authority*
Steven Pinker's *The Better Angels of Our Nature*
Oliver Sacks's *The Man Who Mistook His Wife For a Hat*
Richard Thaler & Cass Sunstein's *Nudge: Improving Decisions About Health, Wealth and Happiness*
Amos Tversky's *Judgment under Uncertainty: Heuristics and Biases*
Philip Zimbardo's *The Lucifer Effect*

SCIENCE

Rachel Carson's *Silent Spring*
William Cronon's *Nature's Metropolis: Chicago And The Great West*
Alfred W. Crosby's *The Columbian Exchange*
Charles Darwin's *On the Origin of Species*
Richard Dawkin's *The Selfish Gene*
Thomas Kuhn's *The Structure of Scientific Revolutions*
Geoffrey Parker's *Global Crisis: War, Climate Change and Catastrophe in the Seventeenth Century*
Mathis Wackernagel & William Rees's *Our Ecological Footprint*

SOCIOLOGY

Michelle Alexander's *The New Jim Crow: Mass Incarceration in the Age of Colorblindness*
Gordon Allport's *The Nature of Prejudice*
Albert Bandura's *Aggression: A Social Learning Analysis*
Hanna Batatu's *The Old Social Classes And The Revolutionary Movements Of Iraq*
Ha-Joon Chang's *Kicking Away the Ladder*
W. E. B. Du Bois's *The Souls of Black Folk*
Émile Durkheim's *On Suicide*
Frantz Fanon's *Black Skin, White Masks*
Frantz Fanon's *The Wretched of the Earth*
Eric Foner's *Reconstruction: America's Unfinished Revolution, 1863-1877*
Eugene Genovese's *Roll, Jordan, Roll: The World the Slaves Made*
Jack Goldstone's *Revolution and Rebellion in the Early Modern World*
Antonio Gramsci's *The Prison Notebooks*
Richard Herrnstein & Charles A Murray's *The Bell Curve: Intelligence and Class Structure in American Life*
Eric Hoffer's *The True Believer: Thoughts on the Nature of Mass Movements*
Jane Jacobs's *The Death and Life of Great American Cities*
Robert Lucas's *Why Doesn't Capital Flow from Rich to Poor Countries?*
Jay Macleod's *Ain't No Makin' It: Aspirations and Attainment in a Low Income Neighborhood*
Elaine May's *Homeward Bound: American Families in the Cold War Era*
Douglas McGregor's *The Human Side of Enterprise*
C. Wright Mills's *The Sociological Imagination*

Thomas Piketty's *Capital in the Twenty-First Century*
Robert D. Putman's *Bowling Alone*
David Riesman's *The Lonely Crowd: A Study of the Changing American Character*
Edward Said's *Orientalism*
Joan Wallach Scott's *Gender and the Politics of History*
Theda Skocpol's *States and Social Revolutions*
Max Weber's *The Protestant Ethic and the Spirit of Capitalism*

THEOLOGY

Augustine's *Confessions*
Benedict's *Rule of St Benedict*
Gustavo Gutiérrez's *A Theology of Liberation*
Carole Hillenbrand's *The Crusades: Islamic Perspectives*
David Hume's *Dialogues Concerning Natural Religion*
Immanuel Kant's *Religion within the Boundaries of Mere Reason*
Ernst Kantorowicz's *The King's Two Bodies: A Study in Medieval Political Theology*
Søren Kierkegaard's *The Sickness Unto Death*
C. S. Lewis's *The Abolition of Man*
Saba Mahmood's *The Politics of Piety: The Islamic Revival and the Feminist Subject*
Baruch Spinoza's *Ethics*
Keith Thomas's *Religion and the Decline of Magic*

COMING SOON

Chris Argyris's *The Individual and the Organisation*
Seyla Benhabib's *The Rights of Others*
Walter Benjamin's *The Work Of Art in the Age of Mechanical Reproduction*
John Berger's *Ways of Seeing*
Pierre Bourdieu's *Outline of a Theory of Practice*
Mary Douglas's *Purity and Danger*
Roland Dworkin's *Taking Rights Seriously*
James G. March's *Exploration and Exploitation in Organisational Learning*
Ikujiro Nonaka's *A Dynamic Theory of Organizational Knowledge Creation*
Griselda Pollock's *Vision and Difference*
Amartya Sen's *Inequality Re-Examined*
Susan Sontag's *On Photography*
Yasser Tabbaa's *The Transformation of Islamic Art*
Ludwig von Mises's *Theory of Money and Credit*

Macat Disciplines

Access the greatest ideas and thinkers across entire disciplines, including

Postcolonial Studies

Roland Barthes's *Mythologies*
Frantz Fanon's *Black Skin, White Masks*
Homi K. Bhabha's *The Location of Culture*
Gustavo Gutiérrez's *A Theology of Liberation*
Edward Said's *Orientalism*
Gayatri Chakravorty Spivak's *Can the Subaltern Speak?*

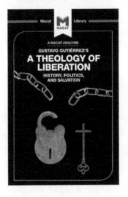

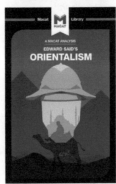

Macat analyses are available from all good bookshops and libraries.

Access hundreds of analyses through one, multimedia tool.
Join free for one month **library.macat.com**

Macat Disciplines

Access the greatest ideas and thinkers across entire disciplines, including

Macat Disciplines

Access the greatest ideas and thinkers across entire disciplines, including

MACAT

FEMINISM, GENDER AND QUEER STUDIES

Simone De Beauvoir's
The Second Sex

Michel Foucault's
History of Sexuality

Betty Friedan's
The Feminine Mystique

Saba Mahmood's
*The Politics of Piety:
The Islamic Revival and
the Feminist Subject*

Joan Wallach Scott's
*Gender and the
Politics of History*

Mary Wollstonecraft's
*A Vindication of the
Rights of Woman*

Virginia Woolf's
A Room of One's Own

Judith Butler's
Gender Trouble

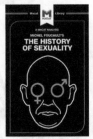

Macat analyses are available from all good bookshops and libraries.

Access hundreds of analyses through one, multimedia tool.
Join free for one month **library.macat.com**

Macat Disciplines

Access the greatest ideas and thinkers across entire disciplines, including

CRIMINOLOGY

Michelle Alexander's
*The New Jim Crow:
Mass Incarceration in the
Age of Colorblindness*

**Michael R. Gottfredson
& Travis Hirschi's**
A General Theory of Crime

Elizabeth Loftus's
Eyewitness Testimony

**Richard Herrnstein
& Charles A. Murray's**
*The Bell Curve: Intelligence and
Class Structure in American Life*

Jay Macleod's
*Ain't No Makin' It:
Aspirations and Attainment in a
Low-Income Neighborhood*

Philip Zimbardo's
The Lucifer Effect

Macat analyses are available from all good bookshops and libraries.

Access hundreds of analyses through one, multimedia tool.
Join free for one month **library.macat.com**

Macat Disciplines

Access the greatest ideas and thinkers across entire disciplines, including

INEQUALITY

Ha-Joon Chang's, *Kicking Away the Ladder*

David Graeber's, *Debt: The First 5000 Years*

Robert E. Lucas's, *Why Doesn't Capital Flow from Rich To Poor Countries?*

Thomas Piketty's, *Capital in the Twenty-First Century*

Amartya Sen's, *Inequality Re-Examined*

Mahbub Ul Haq's, *Reflections on Human Development*

Macat analyses are available from all good bookshops and libraries.

Access hundreds of analyses through one, multimedia tool.
Join free for one month **library.macat.com**

Macat Disciplines

Access the greatest ideas and thinkers across entire disciplines, including

GLOBALIZATION

Arjun Appadurai's, *Modernity at Large: Cultural Dimensions of Globalisation*

James Ferguson's, *The Anti-Politics Machine*

Geert Hofstede's, *Culture's Consequences*

Amartya Sen's, *Development as Freedom*

Macat analyses are available from all good bookshops and libraries.

Access hundreds of analyses through one, multimedia tool.
Join free for one month **library.macat.com**

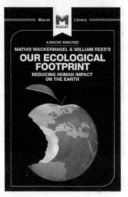

Macat Pairs

*Analyse historical and modern issues from opposite sides of an argument.
Pairs include:*

RACE AND IDENTITY

Zora Neale Hurston's
Characteristics of Negro Expression

Using material collected on anthropological expeditions to the South, Zora Neale Hurston explains how expression in African American culture in the early twentieth century departs from the art of white America. At the time, African American art was often criticized for copying white culture. For Hurston, this criticism misunderstood how art works. European tradition views art as something fixed. But Hurston describes a creative process that is alive, ever-changing, and largely improvisational. She maintains that African American art works through a process called 'mimicry'—where an imitated object or verbal pattern, for example, is reshaped and altered until it becomes something new, novel—and worthy of attention.

Frantz Fanon's
Black Skin, White Masks

Black Skin, White Masks offers a radical analysis of the psychological effects of colonization on the colonized.

Fanon witnessed the effects of colonization first hand both in his birthplace, Martinique, and again later in life when he worked as a psychiatrist in another French colony, Algeria. His text is uncompromising in form and argument. He dissects the dehumanizing effects of colonialism, arguing that it destroys the native sense of identity, forcing people to adapt to an alien set of values—including a core belief that they are inferior. This results in deep psychological trauma.

Fanon's work played a pivotal role in the civil rights movements of the 1960s.

Macat Pairs

Analyse historical and modern issues from opposite sides of an argument. Pairs include:

INTERNATIONAL RELATIONS IN THE 21ˢᵀ CENTURY

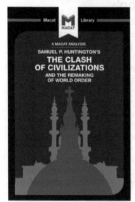

Samuel P. Huntington's
The Clash of Civilisations

In his highly influential 1996 book, Huntington offers a vision of a post-Cold War world in which conflict takes place not between competing ideologies but between cultures. The worst clash, he argues, will be between the Islamic world and the West: the West's arrogance and belief that its culture is a "gift" to the world will come into conflict with Islam's obstinacy and concern that its culture is under attack from a morally decadent "other."

Clash inspired much debate between different political schools of thought. But its greatest impact came in helping define American foreign policy in the wake of the 2001 terrorist attacks in New York and Washington.

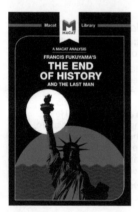

Francis Fukuyama's
The End of History and the Last Man

Published in 1992, *The End of History and the Last Man* argues that capitalist democracy is the final destination for all societies. Fukuyama believed democracy triumphed during the Cold War because it lacks the "fundamental contradictions" inherent in communism and satisfies our yearning for freedom and equality. Democracy therefore marks the endpoint in the evolution of ideology, and so the "end of history." There will still be "events," but no fundamental change in ideology.

Macat Pairs

Analyse historical and modern issues from opposite sides of an argument. Pairs include:

HOW TO RUN AN ECONOMY

John Maynard Keynes's
The General Theory OF Employment, Interest and Money

Classical economics suggests that market economies are self-correcting in times of recession or depression, and tend toward full employment and output. But English economist John Maynard Keynes disagrees.

In his ground-breaking 1936 study *The General Theory*, Keynes argues that traditional economics has misunderstood the causes of unemployment. Employment is not determined by the price of labor; it is directly linked to demand. Keynes believes market economies are by nature unstable, and so require government intervention. Spurred on by the social catastrophe of the Great Depression of the 1930s, he sets out to revolutionize the way the world thinks

Milton Friedman's
The Role of Monetary Policy

Friedman's 1968 paper changed the course of economic theory. In just 17 pages, he demolished existing theory and outlined an effective alternate monetary policy designed to secure 'high employment, stable prices and rapid growth.'

Friedman demonstrated that monetary policy plays a vital role in broader economic stability and argued that economists got their monetary policy wrong in the 1950s and 1960s by misunderstanding the relationship between inflation and unemployment. Previous generations of economists had believed that governments could permanently decrease unemployment by permitting inflation—and vice versa. Friedman's most original contribution was to show that this supposed trade-off is an illusion that only works in the short term.

Macat analyses are available from all good bookshops and libraries.

Access hundreds of analyses through one, multimedia tool.
Join free for one month **library.macat.com**

Macat Pairs

Analyse historical and modern issues from opposite sides of an argument. Pairs include:

ARE WE FUNDAMENTALLY GOOD - OR BAD?

Steven Pinker's
The Better Angels of Our Nature

Stephen Pinker's gloriously optimistic 2011 book argues that, despite humanity's biological tendency toward violence, we are, in fact, less violent today than ever before. To prove his case, Pinker lays out pages of detailed statistical evidence. For him, much of the credit for the decline goes to the eighteenth-century Enlightenment movement, whose ideas of liberty, tolerance, and respect for the value of human life filtered down through society and affected how people thought. That psychological change led to behavioral change—and overall we became more peaceful. Critics countered that humanity could never overcome the biological urge toward violence; others argued that Pinker's statistics were flawed.

Philip Zimbardo's
The Lucifer Effect

Some psychologists believe those who commit cruelty are innately evil. Zimbardo disagrees. In *The Lucifer Effect*, he argues that sometimes good people do evil things simply because of the situations they find themselves in, citing many historical examples to illustrate his point. Zimbardo details his 1971 Stanford prison experiment, where ordinary volunteers playing guards in a mock prison rapidly became abusive. But he also describes the tortures committed by US army personnel in Iraq's Abu Ghraib prison in 2003—and how he himself testified in defence of one of those guards. committed by US army personnel in Iraq's Abu Ghraib prison in 2003—and how he himself testified in defence of one of those guards.

Macat analyses are available from all good bookshops and libraries.

Access hundreds of analyses through one, multimedia tool.
Join free for one month **library.macat.com**

Macat Pairs

Analyse historical and modern issues from opposite sides of an argument. Pairs include:

HOW WE RELATE TO EACH OTHER AND SOCIETY

Jean-Jacques Rousseau's
The Social Contract

Rousseau's famous work sets out the radical concept of the 'social contract': a give-and-take relationship between individual freedom and social order.

If people are free to do as they like, governed only by their own sense of justice, they are also vulnerable to chaos and violence. To avoid this, Rousseau proposes, they should agree to give up some freedom to benefit from the protection of social and political organization. But this deal is only just if societies are led by the collective needs and desires of the people, and able to control the private interests of individuals. For Rousseau, the only legitimate form of government is rule by the people.

Robert D. Putnam's
Bowling Alone

In *Bowling Alone*, Robert Putnam argues that Americans have become disconnected from one another and from the institutions of their common life, and investigates the consequences of this change.

Looking at a range of indicators, from membership in formal organizations to the number of invitations being extended to informal dinner parties, Putnam demonstrates that Americans are interacting less and creating less "social capital" – with potentially disastrous implications for their society.

It would be difficult to overstate the impact of *Bowling Alone*, one of the most frequently cited social science publications of the last half-century.

Macat analyses are available from all good bookshops and libraries.

Access hundreds of analyses through one, multimedia tool.
Join free for one month **library.macat.com**